Ethiopian Cookbook

Traditional Ethiopian Recipes
Made Easy

www.grizzlypublishing.com

Table of Contents

INTRODUCTION 1

BERBERE SPICE 3

TRADITIONAL ETHIOPIAN INJERA FLATBREAD 5

CHAPTER ONE: ETHIOPIAN BREAKFAST RECIPES 7

  ENQULAL FITFIT (ETHIOPIAN SCRAMBLED EGGS) 7
  CHECHEBSA (KITA FIR FIR) 8
  QUANTA FIRFIR 10
  TEFF BREAKFAST BOWL 12
  ETHIOPIAN FUL MEDAMES 14
  FALL VEGETABLE BOWL WITH TEFF DUKKAH 17
  FETIRA 19
  HIMBASHA (ETHIOPIAN CELEBRATION BREAD) 20
  QINCH'É (CRACKED WHEAT) 22
  YEMARINA YEWOTET DABO (ETHIOPIAN HONEY MILK BREAD) ... 24

CHAPTER TWO: ETHIOPIAN LUNCH RECIPES 26

  INGUDAI TIBS (ETHIOPIAN SAUTÉED MUSHROOMS) 26
  MINCHET-ABESH ALICAH (ETHIOPIAN GROUND BEEF STEW) 27
  SHIRO ALECHA 28
  ATKILT WOT/ TIKIL GOMEN (ETHIOPIAN CABBAGE DISH) 29
  AZIFA (GREEN LENTIL SALAD) 31
  GOMEN WAT (ETHIOPIAN SPICED COLLARDS) 32
  YEMISIR WOT (BERBERE LENTILS) 33
  YEKIK ALICHA (ETHIOPIAN SPLIT PEA STEW) - VEGAN GLUTEN FREE 34
  ETHIOPIAN LASAGNA 36
  ETHIOPIAN BUTICHA 38
  ETHIOPIAN POTATO SALAD 39
  KEY SIR ALICHA (ETHIOPIAN BEETS AND POTATOES) 41
  YESHIMBRA ASSA (ETHIOPIAN CHICKPEA "FISH" AND SAUCE) 42
  CHICKEN DRUMSTICKS, ETHIOPIAN STYLE 44
  ASA TIBS FRIED FISH 46
  ETHIOPIAN RED LENTIL BURGERS 47
  ETHIOPIAN CARROT TARTARE 50
  BEG WOT (ETHIOPIAN LAMB STEW) 52
  ETHIOPIAN-STYLE BEEF STIR FRY 54

ETHIOPIAN BEEF TIBS 56

YE'ABESHA GOMEN (ETHIOPIAN COLLARD GREENS) 58

ETHIOPIAN ATAKILT WAT WITH LENTILS AND TOASTED NAAN 59

KIK ALICHA (ETHIOPIAN DAL) 61

GORED GORED (ETHIOPIAN SEASONED CUBED MEAT) 62

ASA BE MITMITA (ETHIOPIAN FRIED FISH WITH MITMITA) 63

CHAPTER THREE: ETHIOPIAN DINNER RECIPES **65**

DORO WOT (ETHIOPIAN CHICKEN STEW) 65

ETHIOPIAN LENTIL STEW - VEGAN 67

ETHIOPIAN BERBERE SPICED CHICKPEAS OVER POLENTA 69

MISR WAT (SPICY ETHIOPIAN RED LENTILS) 71

ETHIOPIAN MEAL 73

DORO TIBS WAT (SPICY ETHIOPIAN CHICKEN) 77

AWAZE TIBS (ETHIOPIAN LAMB & ONION STEW) 78

BERBERE CHICKEN WITH ETHIOPIAN LENTILS 79

BEEF KITFO (ETHIOPIAN TARTARE) WITH INJERA CRISPS 81

YETAKELT W'ET (ETHIOPIAN VEGETABLE STEW WITH BRAISED TEMPEH) 84

ETHIOPIAN SPICY FISH STEW WITH RED ONION 86

BERBERE SPICED CHICKEN BREASTS 87

SEGA WAT (SPICY ETHIOPIAN BEEF STEW) 89

ZIZIL ALICHA WOT (ETHIOPIAN BEEF STEW) 91

WILD MUSHROOM STEW WITH SPICY BERBERE SAUCE 93

ETHIOPIAN FRIED CHICKEN WINGS 95

YE'DIFIN MISSER ALICHA (LENTILS IN GARLIC-GINGER SAUCE RECIPE) - VEGAN GLUTEN-FREE
SOY-FREE 97

YEDORO MINCHET ABISH (SPICY CHICKEN STEW) 99

DULLET (SPICED TRIPE, LIVER AND BEEF) 101

YE QWANT'A ZILBO (DRIED BEEF STEW) 102

MISSIR WOT PIZZA - VEGAN 103

CHAPTER FOUR: ETHIOPIAN DESSERT RECIPES **106**

PUMPKIN SPICE DABO KOLO (ETHIOPIAN PUMPKIN SPICE RICOTTA DONUTS) ... 106

ETHIOPIAN RAS EL HANOUT CRESCENT COOKIES 108

ETHIOPIAN DESTAYE PIEROGIES 111

ETHIOPIAN LENTIL SAMBUSA 116

INJERA BREAD PUDDING 119

ETHIOPIAN FRENCH PRESS AND COCONUT FLOUR BUNDT CAKES - GLUTEN FREE DIARY FREE
.... 120

ETHIOPIAN GRIDDLE CAKES 123

ETHIOPIAN TRUFFLES 126

ETHIOPIAN HONEY WINE 128

CONCLUSION **129**

Introduction

First and foremost, I want to thank you for purchasing this book, 'Ethiopian Cookbook: Traditional Ethiopian Recipes Made Easy.'

Ethiopian is hands down one of the most fascinating cuisines on this planet – and not just because of the food itself! While I will always be the first to admit that traditional Ethiopian cooking is both incredibly unique and ridiculous tasty, I would actually suggest that it is the local food *culture* that truly makes it so amazing.

Ethiopia (once known as Abyssinia, for you history buffs out there) is a country typified by great rocky plateaus and low-lying plains. Historically, the northern high country was once heavily populated by those who held Christian beliefs, while the plains were long home to both local Muslims and Animists – and it was from these religious groups that the Ethiopian cuisine as we know it today evolved.

It has truly become a pure demonstration of their rich history and culture.

Ethiopian food derives its unique and wonderful flavours from the inclusion of its indigenous ingredients, with particular emphasis on red chilies, fenugreek, ginger, and a variety of local spices. These are combined with locally farmed grains, such as millet, sorghum, whole wheat, and the historic Ethiopian 'Teff' (a local Ethiopian grass that produces delicious grains and seeds).

These locally grown ingredients are commonly combined with local meats to produce stews of rich aromatic flavours and unbelievable colour combinations. Trust me when I say that the local cooking is a sight to behold.

Interestingly, in conjunction with their reliance on local grains and spices, Ethiopians have long been revered for their capacity as *beekeepers*.

Over time through this historic local practice, Ethiopians have developed a sound reputation for producing some of the most beautiful honey on the planet – and don't even get me started on their incredible honey wines.

Both of these amazing local ingredients play an important role in the food culture of this incredible country, used in cooking and as a centrepiece of modern-day Ethiopian culture.

But arguably the most important aspect of this amazing cuisine is how it is shared. Ethiopian food is heavily encouraged to be eaten with friends and families. Most commonly served in the form of a shared platter, this deliciously amazing experience is designed with the sole intent to spark conversation and human interaction.

You enter the meal feeling hungry, you leave the meal felling not only full in the belly, but also fulfilled emotionally.

And there is method in this madness.

Before every single meal in you ritually wash your hands. The food is then offered to all those invited on a huge platter, which is draped with delicious breads. All guests eat out of the single platter by simply ripping off a piece of bread and using it to scoop up one the many stews offered.

Honey wine is enjoyed throughout, after which the meal is then finished with another hand wash and a strong expresso.

Absolute perfection.

So, if you are after both a collection of incredibly tasty recipes *and* an amazing culinary experience, I can assure you that you have come to the right place. What are you waiting for? Open the pages and enter a world that is just waiting to be explored.

Berbere Spice

Ingredients:

- 8 black peppercorns
- 5 dried birds' eye (Thai) chilies or dried chili de arbol
- 4 whole cloves
- 2 teaspoons cumin seeds
- 2 teaspoons onion powder
- 1 teaspoon garlic powder
- 1 teaspoon turmeric
- 1 teaspoon fenugreek seeds*
- 1 teaspoon cardamom seeds**
- 1 teaspoon coriander seeds
- ½ teaspoon cayenne pepper
- ½ teaspoon ground ginger
- ¼ cup paprika
- ¼ teaspoon ground nutmeg

Method:

1. In a small, heavy-bottomed skillet over medium heat, add the cumin, fenugreek, cardamom, coriander, cloves, peppercorns, and chilies. Swirling constantly, cook until fragrant, about 3 - 4 minutes.
2. Allow to cool slightly and then add to a spice or coffee grinder. Finely grind.
3. In a small bowl add the spice mixture and the rest of the ingredients. Stir well to combine.
4. Store in an air-tight container for up to 6 months.

Note:

- * While there are a lot of spices in this blend, the only one that you may have trouble finding is, fenugreek. This particular spice has quite a unique flavor, the best way I can describe it is a subtle mixture of celery leaf and maple syrup. Personally, I have not been able to find a decent substitute for the fenugreek, so I would suggest omitting it if you can't find the spice.
- ** You'll want to use cardamom seeds, not the green pods. If all you can find are the pods, simply take a paring knife, slice off the top of the pod and open it up to reveal the black seeds inside.

Traditional Ethiopian Injera Flatbread

Ingredients:

- 4 cups water
- 2 cups teff flour

Method:

1. First, mix 2 cups of teff flour and 3 cups of water together in a large mixing bowl. Cover loosely with a cloth, and allow to ferment for 2 to 3 days until it has a strong sour smell and is beginning to bubble as the fermentation action becomes visible.
2. The mixture will have settled, and there will be a good bit of surface water above a sponge of dough. Without disturbing the sponge below, carefully pour off the surface water.
3. Bring one cup of water to a boil in a saucepan, and add half-cup of the teff sponge to the boiling water. Cook one to two minutes while stirring vigorously with a whisk. Remove from heat and let cool to room temperature.
4. Once the cooked batter has cooled to room temperature, add it back into the raw sourdough batter, stirring to incorporate fully. Add more water to thin the batter to a pourable crepe batter consistency.
5. Cover the batter and allow it to ferment for an additional few hours.
6. Heat a large flat skillet on the stove until very hot. A crepe pan or other flat pan works well. Pour about one-third of a cup of batter onto the pan, and tilt the pan to allow the batter to run and cover the surface in a thin layer.
7. Cook until firm on the first side, noting that when the bubbles pop on the upper side the holes remain open

rather than filling back in. This indicates that it's cooked on the first side. Place a lid on the pan and allow it to cook for another few minutes to steam cook through, because the bread is not flipped.

8. Remove to a plate, and serve your dinner on top of the traditional Ethiopian injera.

Note:

- If you have trouble culturing your own injera with a wild starter from the air, consider adding a bit of yeast or sourdough starter at the beginning, and opt for a shorter fermentation time

Chapter One: Ethiopian Breakfast Recipes

Enqulal Fitfit (Ethiopian Scrambled Eggs)

Serves: 2-3

Ingredients:

- 2 medium-large free-range organic eggs
- 2 tablespoons milk
- 1 fresh green chili
- 1 tomato (finely chopped)
- 1 small onion (finely chopped)
- ½ small green bell pepper (finely chopped)
- ½ small red bell pepper (finely chopped)
- ¼ teaspoon dried powdered garlic
- ¼ teaspoon dried powdered ginger
- salt and pepper to taste

Method:

1. Lightly whisk the eggs with the milk until fluffy. Add all the remaining ingredients except oil and beat well.
2. Heat the oil in a medium frying pan. When hot, add the egg mixture and cook for a few minutes until the omelette is set.
3. Finish the omelette under a grill if desired. Serve hot.

Chechebsa (Kita Fir Fir)

Serves: 3-4

Ingredients:

- 4 tablespoons niter kibbeh (Ethiopian spiced butter)
- 2 tsp *berbere spice*
- 1 ¼ cups all-purpose flour (or 1 cup all-purpose flour and 1/4 cup teff flour)
- 1 tablespoon oil (for frying)
- ½ teaspoon salt
- ¾ cup water (more or less, as needed for consistency)

Method:

1. Heat oil in a large skillet or griddle. Whisk together the flour and salt. Add 1/2 cup water and keep whisking, adding 2 tablespoons more water at a time as needed, and whisking until smooth and the consistency is like a thin pancake batter.
2. Pour the batter into the hot skillet over medium heat. Use the back of a wooden spoon to spread the batter into a single layer to form a large pancake. Cook 2 to 4 minutes or until bottom is lightly browned. Flip the Kita, and cook other side another 1 to 2 minutes or until lightly browned and cooked through. Set the cooked Kita aside for a few minutes, to cool.
3. Tear the Kita into small (about 1 inch) pieces.
4. Add niter kibbeh and berbere to a large skillet, and stir until melted. Add the torn Kita to the skillet and stir well with a wooden spoon until all the pieces are well coated with the spicy butter. Cook for several minutes, or until heated throughout.

5. It should be moist but not mashed (more like the consistency of a savory bread pudding or a moist bread-based stuffing).
6. Spoon into individual bowls and serve immediately with a spoon while still warm.

Quanta Firfir

Serves: 2

Ingredients:

- 2-3 ounces beef jerky, chopped into 1/4-inch pieces (use only plain jerky; not anything flavored, like teriyaki)
- 6 cloves garlic
- 3 big handfuls fully-dried injera that has been torn up into bite-size pieces
- 2 tablespoons berbere spice
- 2 cups water
- 2 medium onions (chopped)
- 1 teaspoon salt
- ¼ cup vegetable oil
- fresh injera for serving
- a couple hard-boiled eggs, peeled (optional)

Method:

1. First, heat a dry saucepan over medium heat.
2. Add onions and sweat them, without any oil, until they become translucent, about 5 minutes.
3. Add oil and sauté another couple minute.
4. Add half the garlic and sauté yet another couple minutes.
5. Add berbere and continue to sauté.
6. The mixture will start to stick.
7. When it does, add a couple tablespoons of the water.
8. Repeat this process until you only have ¾ of a cup of water left.
9. Then add the water, the rest of the garlic, beef jerky, and salt and immediately remove the pan from the heat and let rest for 60 seconds.

10. Now stir in the injera chips very gently, so as not to break them.
11. Continue to stir gently until all the liquid is absorbed.
12. The injera should be pretty spongy, so if it isn't, stir in a bit more water.
13. Serve with the eggs on top and fresh injera.

Teff Breakfast Bowl

Serves: 3

Ingredients:

- 1 cup teff grains (not the flour – unless you prefer a smoother texture)
- 1 stick cinnamon
- ½ teaspoon cloves
- ½ teaspoon cardamom
- 2/3 cup water
- 2/3 cup almond milk

Toppings:

- 6 teaspoon maple syrup
- 3 tablespoons almond butter
- 1 ½ pears (sliced)
- ½ cup pecans

Method:

1. Start by adding the teff, water, almond milk, cinnamon, cloves and cardamom to a pot and bring to a boil. Be sure to stir frequently. As it begins to thicken, turn the heat down and put a lid on the pot until it's cooked all the way through.
2. Pour 1/3 of the teff mix into a bowl and remove the cloves, cinnamon and cardamom.
3. Top the teff bowl with half a thinly sliced pear, 1/3 of the pecans, 1 tablespoon almond butter and 2 teaspoon maple syrup.

4. Pour the remaining teff mix evenly into two bowls and repeat the topping steps above (or refrigerate and enjoy as two days' worth of pre-made breakfast).

Ethiopian Ful Medames

Serves: 4

Ingredients:

Ful medames:

- 400g of fava beans (tinned, or mixed beans if you can't find them)
- 100ml of stock
- 2 garlic cloves (minced)
- 1 onion (finely diced)
- 1 teaspoon berbere

Niter kibbeh:

- 250g of unsalted butter
- 4 black cardamom pods (crushed)
- 2 garlic cloves (sliced)
- 1 shallot (finely diced)
- 1 knob of ginger (sliced)
- 1 cinnamon stick
- 1 teaspoon cumin seeds
- 1 teaspoon fenugreek seeds
- 1 teaspoon coriander seeds
- 1 teaspoon black peppercorns
- 1 bay leaf

Mitmita:

- 2 tablespoons of dried bird's eye chilies
- 1 teaspoon salt
- 1 teaspoon cardamom pod
- ½ teaspoon cloves

To serve:

- 2 medium-large eggs (soft boiled for 6 minutes, peeled and halved)
- 1 plum tomato (finely diced)
- 1 spring onion (finely sliced)
- 1 handful of parsley (chopped)
- crusty bread rolls

Method:

1. Begin by making the niter kibbeh.
2. Place all the ingredients in a pan and slowly simmer for 15–20 minutes. When the solids in the butter start to caramelize, strain the butter through a muslin cloth or coffee filter.
3. The niter kibbeh can now be kept refrigerated for up to 2 weeks.
4. For the ful medames, heat 3 tablespoons of niter kibbeh and gently sauté the diced onion, garlic and berbere spice until soft, about 5 minutes.
5. Drain the beans and add to the pan with the stock. Simmer on a low heat until the stock has nearly all evaporated and the beans can be mashed with the back of a wooden spoon.
6. As you wait for the beans to cook, prepare the mitmita spice blend. Toast the chilies, cardamom and cloves in a hot dry pan until fragrant. Transfer them to a spice grinder with the salt and blend to a powder.
7. The mitmita can now be kept in an airtight container for 3 months, though is best used within 2 weeks for a more vibrant flavor.

8. Spread out the roughly mashed beans onto a serving plate and drizzle with some more niter kibbeh. Top with the boiled eggs, tomato, spring onion and parsley.
9. Serve with a sprinkling of mitmita and some crusty white bread rolls.

Fall Vegetable Bowl with Teff Dukkah

Serves: 4

Ingredients:

- 3 cups cooked wild and brown rice mix
- 2 cups steamed spinach
- 2 tablespoons olive oil
- 2 teaspoon ground turmeric
- 2 tablespoons fresh lemon juice
- 2 tablespoons each fennel seeds and cumin seeds
- 1½ cups cooked chickpeas
- 1 teaspoon sea salt, divided
- 1 cup unsweetened full-fat or coconut-milk yogurt
- 1 large head cauliflower (cut into florets)
- 1/2 cup teff
- ½ cup shelled pistachios (toasted and finely chopped)
- ½ teaspoon minced garlic
- ¼ cup toasted sesame seeds

Method:

1. Add teff to a large sauté pan on medium-low heat. Toast for about 2 to 3 minutes, until teff begins to make popping sounds. Stir in ¾ cup water, reduce heat to low and cover. Cook for 5 to 6 minutes, or until water is fully evaporated, then remove from heat. Let sit, covered, for 5 minutes longer, then spread out teff on a baking sheet to dry.

2. In a small sauté pan, toast fennel and cumin seeds for 2 to 3 minutes, until fragrant. Use a spice grinder or mortar and pestle to grind into a powder. Mix together dried teff,

pistachios, ground spices, sesame seeds and ¾ teaspoon salt. Set aside until ready to use.

3. Mix together yogurt, lemon juice, garlic and 1/8 teaspoon salt. Refrigerate until ready to use.

4. Preheat oven to 450°F. In a bowl, toss cauliflower, chickpeas, oil, turmeric and remaining 1/8 teaspoon salt; spread onto a baking sheet. Roast for 25-30 minutes, tossing 2 to 3 times during cooking, until well browned.

5. To assemble, fill each bowl with ¾ cup rice and drizzle 3 tablespoons yogurt mixture and 2 tablespoons dukkah. Divide cauliflower-chickpea mixture and spinach on top. Drizzle each with 1 tbsp yogurt and top with 1 to 2 tablespoons more dukkah (use more to taste). Serve warm or cool.

Note:

- This recipe makes about double the amount of dukkah you will need for the bowls. Store remaining dukkah in the refrigerator for up to 1 week and in the freezer for up to 1 month. Use as a garnish for just about any savory dish from salads to soups to cooked mains.

Fetira

Serves: 6-8

Ingredients:

- 200 g (1 ¼ cups) white flour (plus more for dusting)
- 150 ml (½ cup) salted water
- butter (enough to spread over the dough)
- sunflower oil (just enough to cover the pan every time you cook the fetira)

Garnish:

- Maple syrup

Method:

1. In a big bowl mix the flour and water till you make a dough.
2. Take it out on your working border and stretch it out thinly.
3. Picking a little butter with your fingers spread it all over the rolled-out pasta.
4. Tear the pasta right at the center and fold it towards the outside and make a circle
5. Smash it against the working border so that it gets lose and fluffy.
6. Cut the dough in 6-8 equal sizes.
7. Roll out each one to a small disk, spread some butter again fold all the edges to the center and roll it out again.
8. Heat a nonstick pan with a little bit of oil and cook till golden brown about 2 minutes on each.
9. Drizzle some maple syrup and enjoy.

Himbasha (Ethiopian Celebration Bread)

Serves: 2-4

Ingredients:

- 5 tablespoons canola oil
- 4-5 cups flour
- 2 teaspoons white sugar
- 1 medium-large egg
- 1 teaspoon salt
- 1 cup warm milk (whole milk is best)
- 1 tablespoon dry active yeast
- 1/3 cup white sugar
- ¼ cup warm water
- 1 teaspoon nigella seeds (optional)

Method:

1. First, combine yeast, water and 2 teaspoons sugar in a small bowl. Allow to proof for 5-10 minutes.
2. Whisk together the egg, sugar, nigella seeds (optional) and salt in a large bowl until smooth.
3. Add the yeast mixture, warmed milk and canola oil. Whisk until well blended.
4. Add flour slowly about a half cup at a time until the mixture forms a soft dough. When the dough is still sticky, but doesn't stick to the edge of the bowl, it's ready to knead.
5. Place the dough on a floured surface and knead adding flour as necessary. This takes 5-6 minutes. Your dough should feel soft and elastic, but not stick to the board or your hands when you are finished.

6. Spray a large stainless steel or glass bowl with non-stick cooking spray. Place the dough in the bowl and turn it to ensure all sides are covered in oil. This will prevent the dough from drying out.
7. Cover with plastic wrap and then a tea towel and place in a warm location until it doubles in size. This takes about 90 minutes.
8. Punch down the dough a few times to remove air bubbles.
9. Grease a 14" round cake pan or large pizza pan (preferably one with higher sides). Place the dough onto the pan and press into a round.
10. Cover with a tea towel, return to warm location and let rise for 30 minutes – 1 hour.
11. With a butter knife, cut into sections and decorate as desired.
12. Bake at 325°F for 35-45 minutes or until the top is crusty and light golden brown.
13. Remove from the oven and lightly brush with butter.
14. Cut into 2-3-inch pieces and serve.

Notes:

- Just before the Himbasha goes into the oven to rise, turn the oven on to 170°F for about 1 minute and then shut it off immediately. The oven then retains enough heat for the rising process.
- The Nigella seeds make this sweet bread a little bit more savory.

Qinch'e (Cracked Wheat)

Serves: 8

Ingredients:

Qinch'e:

- 1 cup milk
- 1/2 cup water
- pinch salt
- 1 cup bulgur wheat
- 4 oz *nit'ir qibe (see below)*

Nit'ir Qibe:

- 4 oz of ghee (clarified butter)
- 2 small cardamom pods
- 1 tablespoon minced ginger
- 1 small clove of garlic (chopped)
- 1 small shallot (chopped)
- ¼ teaspoon fenugreek seeds
- ¼ teaspoon cumin seeds
- ¼ teaspoon oregano
- dash of turmeric

Method:

For the Nit'ir Qibe:

1. Melt ghee at low heat.
2. Add all the remaining ingredients and cook at low heat for 15 minutes, stirring frequently.
3. Strain the nit'ir qibe before using or storing.

For the Qinch'e:

1. Start by bringing the water, milk, and salt to a boil, stirring to ensure they do not separate.
2. Add bulgur wheat and strained nit'ir qibe; continue to stir frequently.
3. The butter will separate and be on the surface at the beginning. As the wheat cooks the butter will suddenly be absorbed.
4. Once the butter has been absorbed, continue to cook the qinch'e until it reaches the desired consistency.

Yemarina Yewotet Dabo (Ethiopian Honey Milk Bread)

Serves: 1 loaf

Ingredients:

- 4 tablespoons unsalted butter (melted and cooled slightly)
- 4 ½ cups all-purpose flour (divided)
- 1 ½ teaspoons salt
- 1 teaspoon sugar or honey
- 1 tablespoon active dry yeast
- 1 medium-large egg
- 1 tablespoon ground coriander
- 1 cup warm whole milk
- ½ cup mild honey
- ½ teaspoon ground cinnamon
- ¼ teaspoon ground cloves
- ¼ cup lukewarm water
- 1/8 teaspoon ground ginger

Method:

1. Using a small bowl, stir together water, 1 teaspoon sugar or honey, and ginger. Sprinkle with yeast, let sit for a minute, then stir to combine. Let sit until frothy, about 10 minutes.
2. In the bowl of a large food processor fitted with a dough blade or a large bowl, add the egg, ½ cup honey, coriander, cinnamon, cloves, salt, milk, butter, and 1 cup of flour.

3. Pour in the frothy yeast mixture and process or mix until thoroughly combined. Slowly add the remaining flour, ½ cup at a time, until a soft dough comes together.
4. On a lightly floured surface, knead dough until smooth and elastic, about 5 minutes. Try not to add anymore flour.
5. Oil a large bowl and add the dough, turning to coat. Cover and let rise until doubled, about 1-2 hours.
6. Heavily grease a 3-inch-deep 3-quart round baking dish or 10-inch springform pan with butter.
7. Punch down the dough and knead a few times before forming into a ball and placing in greased pan, pressing down to cover the bottom. Cover and let rise until the dough reach the top of the pan, about 1 hour.
8. Preheat oven to 300 degrees F when the dough is almost finished rising. Bake in preheated oven until the top is golden brown, about 1 hour.
9. Let it rest in pan for about 5 minutes before removing to a wire rack to cool.
10. Serve.

Chapter Two: Ethiopian Lunch Recipes

Ingudai Tibs (Ethiopian Sautéed Mushrooms)

Serves: 4-6

Ingredients:

- 10-12 medium sized cremini mushrooms (sliced into strips)
- 4 cloves garlic (finely minced)
- 3 tablespoons of berbere spice
- 3 tablespoons oil
- 1 2-inch piece of ginger (peeled then finely minced)
- 1 tablespoon water
- ½ an onion (julienned)
- ½ medium-large tomato (cut into wedges)
- salt, pepper, dried or fresh parsley

Method:

1. First, heat the oil in a pan or skillet over medium heat. Add the julienned onion, tossing to coat with the oil. Cook just until the onions starts becoming tender (1-2 minutes).
2. Add the sliced mushrooms. Cook until the mushrooms start turning color (1-2 minutes), then add the tomato wedges. Add the minced garlic and ginger.
3. Stir together the berbere spice and water, until you form a thick paste. Stir the paste into the mushroom mixture, until everything is evenly coated.
4. Add a pinch of salt, pinch of pepper, and a generous pinch of parsley. Cook for 10-15 minutes until the mushrooms are fully cooked.
5. Serve with injera.

Minchet-Abesh Alicah (Ethiopian Ground Beef Stew)

Serves: 2-4

Ingredients:

- 1 lb. ground lean beef
- 4 cup water (boiled)
- 1 teaspoon garlic powder or garlic cloves (diced)
- 1 cup onion (thinly chopped)
- ½ cup ghee
- ¼ cup white wine (if preferred)
- ¼ teaspoon cardamom powder (korerima)
- ¼ ginger powder or 1 tablespoon fresh ginger juice
- ¼ teaspoon turmeric or curry
- ¼ teaspoon white pepper powder
- salt and pepper to taste

Method:

1. Sauté the onion in medium pot using one cup of boiled water by adding two tablespoon each time until the onion is soft and golden brown.
2. In the cooked onion, add one cup boiled water, ghee, garlic, ginger, wine and turmeric. Cook for 5 minutes.
3. Spread the ground beef on a baking pan and cook it in oven or stir-fry until brown.
4. Sprinkle the stir-fry ground beef in the sauce, mix well. Add two cups boiled water, cover and cook it for about 20 minutes.
5. Add to the stew white pepper, salt and cardamom, cook it for about 5 minutes, remove from heat.
6. Serve with injera bread or white rice.

Shiro Alecha

Serves: 1-2

Ingredients:

- 1 tablespoon turmeric
- 1 onion (chopped)
- 1 tablespoon ginger (minced)
- 1 tablespoon garlic (minced)
- ½ cup oil
- 2-3 cup water
- ¾ cup shiro
- salt, to taste
- 1 jalapeño pepper, deseeded and sliced into thin strips (optional)

Method:

1. Start with cooking the onions dry in a large pan or wok, stirring frequently, for several minutes on medium-high heat. When the onions have softened, add the oil.
2. When the oil has heated through, add the turmeric and mix well. Simmer a few minutes, then add 2 cups of water and bring to a boil.
3. Add the shiro slowly and stir briskly (preferably with a whisk) to remove any lumps. Add more water or oil as needed and continue cooking. Add the ginger and garlic and salt, if desired, and stir.
4. Serve.

Atkilt Wot/ Tikil Gomen (Ethiopian Cabbage Dish)

Serves: 4-6

Ingredients:

- a head of cabbage (finely chopped)
- 3 cups of potatoes (chopped)
- 4 cloves garlic (minced)
- 2 medium-large carrots (sliced)
- 2 teaspoons extra virgin olive oil or coconut oil
- 2 teaspoon ginger (minced)
- 1 medium sized onion (chopped)
- 1 teaspoon turmeric powder
- 1/2 teaspoon cumin powder
- 1/2 teaspoon fenugreek seeds
- 1/2 teaspoon cardamom powder
- 1/2 teaspoon cinnamon powder
- 1/4 teaspoon powdered cloves

Method:

1. Start making your atkilt wot by warming the oil in a large skillet, then adding the garlic, onion and ginger.
2. For a little extra heat, consider adding in a chopped green chili at this stage. Cook these for 5 minutes, or until the onions start looking translucent. Add in the spices and mix up while cooking for another 2 minutes.
3. Next, add the carrots, potato and cabbage and mix well, adding a ¼ teaspoon of salt. Cover and cook for a further 15 minutes, stirring a couple of times to avoid excess browning.
4. Don't add water! The liquid from the vegetables will stay in the pan under the cover and help to keep things nice

and moist. Add a little extra salt to taste, along with a generous amount of black pepper and a little extra oil if you feel it is necessary.

5. Cook until the vegetables are tender.

Note:

- Be sure to chop your garlic first as certain compounds in garlic undergo a chemical change when exposed to air that helps protect them from heat, meaning you get more of the healthy benefits of garlic if you chop it around 15 minutes before cooking.

Azifa (Green Lentil Salad)

Serves: 4

Ingredients:

- 5 tablespoons olive oil
- 4 tablespoons fresh lemon juice
- 2 medium-large tomatoes (peeled and chopped)
- 1 cup (8 oz) green lentil (soaked overnight)
- 1 red onion (finely chopped)
- 1 green chili pepper (seeded and chopped)
- ½ teaspoon prepared mustard
- salt & freshly ground black pepper to taste

Method:

1. Prepare a saucepan and place the lentils, cover with water and bring to a boil.
2. Simmer for about 45 minutes until soft, drain, then turn into a bowl and mash lightly with a potato masher.
3. Add the remaining ingredients and mix well. Adjust seasonings to taste.
4. Chill before serving.

Gomen Wat (Ethiopian Spiced Collards)

Serves: 2-3

Ingredients:

- 2 pounds collards (stemmed and chopped into long strips)
- 3 tablespoons ghee or coconut oil
- 3-4 cloves garlic (chopped finely)
- 1 ½ cups water
- 1 tablespoon black cardamom seeds
- 1 tablespoon ground allspice
- 1 tablespoon cumin seeds
- 1 medium-large sweet onion (chopped)
- 1 tablespoon ground clove
- ½ teaspoon smoked paprika
- ¼ cup rose or white wine vinegar
- 1/8 teaspoon cayenne
- salt and pepper to taste

Method:

1. Dry toast cardamom, allspice, and cumin in a medium pot for about 2 minutes over low heat. Add ghee and fry 2 minutes more.
2. Add onion and garlic, cooking until soft and slightly translucent.
3. Add collards, clove, paprika, cayenne, and water and cook 40-55 minutes over medium heat, until most of the water has evaporated and the collards are completely soft.
4. Top with vinegar, salt and pepper to taste, and serve hot. Enjoy!

Yemisir Wot (Berbere Lentils)

Serves: 3-4

Ingredients:

- ¾ cup (185 mL) canola oil
- 1 ½ medium yellow onions (finely chopped)
- ½ cup (125 mL) *berbere spice* (or to taste)
- 1 tablespoon (15 mL) puréed fresh ginger (peeled)
- 2 teaspoon (10 mL) puréed fresh garlic
- 1 cup (250 mL) dried red lentils (washed)
- 3 cups (750 mL) water (plus more if needed)
- ½ teaspoon (2 mL) fine sea salt (or to taste)

Method:

1. Prepare a medium saucepan and heat oil over medium heat. Add onions. Cook and stir for about 8 minutes.
2. Put in the berbere, ginger and garlic. Cook, stirring, about 2 minutes.
3. Add the lentils. Cook, stirring, 1 minute.
4. Add 3 cups (750 mL) water. Bring to boil over high heat. Reduce heat to medium-low. Simmer, stirring often and adding water if needed, until lentils disintegrate and mixture is a thick stew, about 30 minutes.
5. Taste; season with salt.

Yekik Alicha (Ethiopian Split Pea Stew) - Vegan Gluten free

Serves: 2

Ingredients:

- ¼ cup dry split yellow peas soak overnight or 2 hours
- ¼ cup dry split green peas soak overnight or 2 hours
- 4-5 garlic cloves (minced)
- 2 teaspoons ginger (minced)
- 2 teaspoons oil
- 1 ½ cups water
- ½ red onion (chopped)
- 1/3 teaspoon turmeric powder
- salt and pepper to taste

Variations:

- Add a 1/2 teaspoon berbere spice blend for a spicier Wat version
- Add a chopped Serrano pepper.

Method:

1. First, soak the split peas overnight or at least 2 hours in warm water, drain and rinse.
2. In a deep pan, add oil, add onions, ginger and garlic and cook stirring occasionally, until translucent. (add chopped Serrano or Jalapeno if using)
3. Add the turmeric and mix well.
4. Add rinsed split peas, salt, pepper and water. Mix, cover and bring to a boil on medium heat.

5. Reduce heat to low and simmer, partially covered for 35-45 minutes or until peas have softened to your desired consistency. Taste and adjust salt and spice if needed.

6. *Or use a Pressure cooker:* Pressure cook for 1 whistle on high and then on low for 15 minutes. (Pressure cook for 8 to 10 minutes after the pressure is reached for electric pressure cooker, then natural release). The pictures are of the pressure-cooked stew.

7. Mash the peas if desired. Add some lemon juice if desired and serve. Tastes best with a sour flat bread like Injera.

Ethiopian Lasagna

Serves: 8-10

Ingredients:

- 1 ½ lb. lean ground beef
- 2 15-ounce cans of tomato sauce
- 8 cloves of garlic (minced)
- 4 cups shredded mozzarella (divided)
- 2 cups shredded orange cheddar
- 2 medium-large fresh tomatoes (chopped)
- 2 green onions (thinly sliced)
- 2 bay leaves
- 2 tablespoons dried oregano
- 2 tablespoons fresh basil (chopped)
- 1 tablespoon smoked paprika
- 1 tablespoon ground coriander seeds
- 1 box lasagna noodles
- 1 medium-large onion (diced)
- 1 tablespoon tomato paste
- ½ cup grated parmesan
- ¼ cup extra virgin olive oil
- berbere to taste

Method:

1. First, heat olive oil in a heavy-bottomed pot or Dutch oven over medium heat. Add onions and allow to allow to sweat for about 3 minutes, then stir in tomatoes, garlic, and green onions. Cook for 3-5 more minutes.
2. Add beef to the pot, being careful to break up clumps with wooden spoon. Add salt and pepper to taste, then cook until meat is browned, about 10 minutes. If you prefer a

less clumpy sauce, add about 4 oz. water to the meat mixture as it cooks.

3. Add tomato paste and berbere to pot; allow to cook for 5 minutes before adding tomato sauce, paprika, coriander, bay leaves, oregano, and basil. Reduce heat and simmer for up to 2 hours, stirring occasionally.

4. Pre-heat oven to 375 degrees and grease glass casserole pan. Boil lasagna noodles in a large pot of salted water, until just shy of al dente—about 7 or 8 minutes. Drain and set aside.

5. Immediately before beginning to layer the lasagna, stir 1 cup of mozzarella directly into the sauce mix.

6. Ladle meat sauce mixture directly onto the pan, spreading to cover evenly. Follow with a layer of noodles, then sauce, then both cheeses. Continue alternating until the lasagna is constructed.

7. Sprinkle parmesan over the top layer of mozzarella and cheddar, then cover lasagna with a layer cooking spray-treated aluminum foil. Bake covered for 45 minutes at 475, then remove foil and bake for another 15 minutes or until a significant portion of the top cheese layer has browned.

8. Allow to cool at least 30 minutes before slicing.

Ethiopian Buticha

Serves: 1-2

Ingredients:

- 2 tablespoons olive oil
- 1 cup chickpeas (cooked)
- 1 teaspoon mustard
- 1 teaspoon Jalapeno or red chili pepper flakes
- 1 cup water
- ½ cup red onion
- ½ Lemon (juiced)
- salt and pepper to taste

Method:

1. Place all ingredients in a blender and blend until a smooth, pasty consistency is achieved.
2. Put in container with a lid and place in the refrigerator, to chill, for about one hour before serving.
3. Serve with bread or Ethiopian Injera.

Ethiopian Potato Salad

Serves: 4-6

Ingredients:

- 1 lb. russet potatoes or 1 lb. white potato (scrubbed, peeled)
- 2 -3 tablespoons grapeseed oil
- 2 tablespoons fresh flat-leaf Italian parsley, chopped (NOT dried)
- 1 lemon (juiced, to taste)
- 1/3 cup white onion (finely minced)
- salt and pepper to taste
- 1 green jalapeno pepper, minced (optional)

Method:

1. Start by cutting the potatoes into 2-2 1/2" chunks.
2. Bring a large pot of water to boil and add the potatoes.
3. Cook about 20 minutes or until fork tender.
4. Drain. Rinse potatoes under cold water to stop the cooking process.
5. Set aside to cool.
6. In serving bowl combine the oil, white onion, Italian parsley, salt, pepper and jalapeno if using. Add the cooled potatoes, breaking up the chunks into smaller bite sized pieces and tossing with the oil and onion mixture.
7. Refrigerate at least 3 hours. Keep chilled until just before serving.
8. Adjust seasonings, adding more lemon juice, etc. if necessary.

Note:

- This potato salad is intended to be scooped up using traditional Ethiopian injera bread or use another similar flatbread such as pita, flour tortillas, chapatis, etc.

Key Sir Alicha (Ethiopian Beets and Potatoes)

Serves: 4

Ingredients:

- 4 medium-large potatoes (diced)
- 2 large beets (diced)
- 1 ½ teaspoons fresh garlic (minced)
- 1 cup water (or more as needed)
- 1 yellow onion (diced)
- ½ teaspoon salt (divided, or as needed)
- ¼ cup canola oil
- 1 ½ teaspoons minced fresh ginger (optional)

Method:

1. Prepare a large pot and heat oil over medium heat; add onion and a pinch of salt. Cook and stir onion until softened and translucent, about 5-10 minutes. Add garlic and ginger; cook and stir until fragrant, about 1 minute.
2. Add beets and stir to combine. Pour water over beet mixture and sprinkle ½ teaspoon salt; bring to a boil.
3. Cover pot and reduce heat to medium-low; simmer, stirring occasionally, until beets are easily pierced with a fork, 20 to 25 minutes. Add potatoes and cook until potatoes are soft but not falling apart, about 15 minutes.
4. Serve with bread or Ethiopian Injera.

Yeshimbra Assa (Ethiopian Chickpea "Fish" And Sauce)

Serves: 4-6

Ingredients:

- 3 cups chickpea flour
- 2 teaspoons salt
- 2 tablespoons onions (finely grated)
- 1 teaspoon garlic (finely chopped)
- 1 teaspoon white pepper
- ¾ - 1 cup water
- vegetable oil (for frying)

For the sauce:

- 2 cups onions (finely chopped)
- 1 ½ cups water
- 1 teaspoon salt
- 1 tablespoon garlic (finely chopped)
- ½ cup berbere
- ¼ cup vegetable oil

Method:

1. First, sift the flour, 2 teaspoons of salt and the white pepper into a deep bowl.
2. Make a well in the center and combine ¾ cup water, the onions and garlic in the well.
3. Gradually stir the dry ingredients into the water and onions and, when blended, beat vigorously with a spoon or knead with your hands until the dough is smooth and can be gathered into a ball.

4. If the dough crumbles, add up to ¼ cup water, 1 teaspoon at a time, until the dough comes together.
5. On a lightly floured surface, roll out the dough until it is about ¼ inch thick.
6. With a small sharp knife, cut the dough into fish shapes about 3 inches long and 1 inch wide. If you like, you can use the point of the knife to decorate the top of each "fish" with scales and fins.
7. Pour oil into a deep fryer or a large, heavy saucepan to a depth of 2-3 inches.
8. Heat until it reaches 350 F and fry the "fish" for 3-4 minutes, turning them frequently until they puff slightly and are golden brown.
9. As they brown, transfer them to paper towels to drain.
10. Once you are done the fish you can make the sauce.
11. In a heavy 10-12-inch-wide pan (it's best if it's non-stick), cook the chopped onions for 5-6 minutes until they are soft and dry.
12. Pour in the ¼ cup oil and when it's hot, add the berbere and garlic and stir for a minute.
13. Pour in the 1 ½ cups water and cook until the sauce is slightly thickened.
14. Season with salt and then place the "fish" in the skillet and baste them with the sauce.
15. Lower the heat, cover the pan and simmer for 30 minutes.
16. To serve, arrange the "fish" on a platter and pour the sauce over them.

Chicken Drumsticks, Ethiopian Style

Serves: 7

Ingredients:

- 3-4 pounds chicken legs, thighs or wings
- 2 tablespoons peanut oil, or melted butter (or ghee)
- lemons or limes for serving
- salt to taste

Spice mix:

- 2 tablespoons sweet paprika
- 1 tablespoon hot paprika, or 1-2 teaspoons cayenne
- 2 teaspoons garlic powder
- 1 teaspoon ground ginger
- 1 teaspoon ground cumin
- 1 teaspoon onion powder
- 1 teaspoon black pepper
- 1 teaspoon ground fenugreek
- 1/2 teaspoon salt
- 1/2 teaspoon ground cardamom
- 1/4 teaspoon ground cloves

Method:

1. Start by preheat your oven to 325°. Coat the drumsticks in the peanut oil or melted butter, then sprinkle with salt.
2. Mix all the spices together in a small bowl. In a large bowl, mix half of the spice mix with the chicken, then arrange the drumsticks in a casserole dish lined with enough foil to make a package; you will be cooking these legs covered for most of the time.

3. Sprinkle more of the spice mix over the drumsticks. You can use all of the spice mix, or stop whenever you want. The more mix, the spicier the chicken. Fold over the foil to seal up the drumsticks and bake for 90 minutes.

4. At 90 minutes, open up the foil packet to let the chicken continue to cook uncovered. Continue cooking for at least another 15 minutes, and as long as you like. I like the meat to almost fall off the bone on my drumsticks, so I cook uncovered for another 30-45 minutes.

5. To serve, baste with a little of the sauce that forms at the bottom of the pan, and use the rest to flavor some rice or flatbread. Squeeze some lemon or lime juice over the chicken right before you serve it. A green salad is a good side dish, too.

Asa Tibs Fried Fish

Serves: 7

Ingredients:

- 2 pounds monkfish (or your favorite white flesh fish)
- 1 1/2 tablespoons berbere
- salt, to taste
- oil, for frying
- 1 thinly sliced onion
- 2 finely chopped garlic cloves
- 3 finely chopped small chilis
- juice of 1 lime

Method:

1. Start by sprinkling berbere over fish and leave for 1 hour to marinate.
2. Heat enough oil in a large skillet for deep frying. Add fish pieces and fry until golden on all sides and cooked through. Remove to a paper towel lined plate to absorb excess oil. Sprinkle with a little salt.
3. Add onions and cook until golden and caramelized, about 10 minutes. Most of the oil will have evaporated. Add garlic and chilis. Cook for 1 more minute.
4. Return fish to the pan. Add lime juice and toss to combine.
5. Serve with lime and an extra garnish of more berbere.

Ethiopian Red Lentil Burgers

Serves: 6

Ingredients:

- 1 cup red lentils, rinsed *(see note)*
- 4 tablespoons extra virgin olive oil (plus more for brushing)
- 1 medium red onion (diced)
- 4 cloves garlic (minced)
- 1 teaspoon fresh ginger (grated)
- 2 tablespoons *berbere spice*
- ½ - 1 teaspoon kosher salt
- 2 cups water
- 1 lime (juiced)
- 1 medium egg (beaten)
- ¾ cup panko bread crumbs

Suggested toppings:

- cheese
- lettuce
- tomato
- red onion
- mayonnaise
- mustard

Method:

1. Prepare a pot, add water and bring to a boil. Add the lentils and cook according to the package directions, though leave them a little al dente, as they will simmer in a spiced liquid a little later in the recipe. About 5 -10

minutes, depending on the size of the lentils. Drain the lentils and set aside.

2. Warm the olive oil in a large sauté pan over medium heat. Add the onion and cook until softened, about 5 minutes. Add the garlic and ginger, cook for 2 minutes. Stir in the berbere to form a paste.

3. Add the lentils, ½ teaspoon of salt, and water. Bring to a simmer for 10 minutes, until most of the water has evaporated and the mixture has thickened into a stew-like consistency. Taste and add more salt, if needed. Finish with fresh lime juice and allow to simmer for 5 more minutes.

4. Allow to cool a bit and then stir in the egg and panko bread crumbs.

5. Scoop a ½ cup of the mixture into your hand and form into a patty, approximately the same diameter as the buns. Place the completed burgers on a plate and refrigerate for 10 minutes - this will help them firm up so they don't fall apart while on the grill.

6. While the burgers are in the fridge, heat your grill to medium-high if using gas. If using charcoal, build a medium-hot fire. (Be sure to clean and oil your grill). Alternatively, you can heat a cast-iron pan over medium-high heat. You can also try baking them instead - set your oven to 350 degrees, and bake for about 8-10 minutes.

7. Brush the tops of the burgers with olive oil, place them oiled side down on the grill, and then brush the other side with oil (do not press them into the grill with your spatula). Allow to cook, undisturbed for 3 minutes on each side. (When you're flipping or moving the burgers, be gentle. They're a little more fragile than something like a beef burger).

8. Once all of the burgers have been cooked, be sure to brush the inside of each split hamburger bun with olive oil and toast on the grill for a few minutes, just until golden-brown and crispy.

9. To plate, place the burger on the bottom bun, add whatever toppings and condiments you like. Serve immediately and enjoy!

Note:

- If you're looking for red lentils in your grocery store, try the international aisle if you cannot find them with the other legumes. If you still can't find them, I've used both brown and green lentils as a substitute and the taste is still great! Just be aware that you'll need to boil them longer initially. For that, I recommend following the package directions.

Ethiopian Carrot Tartare

Serves: 4-6

Ingredients:

- 3 medium carrots (peeled)
- 5-6 tablespoons unsalted butter
- ½ teaspoon ground cardamom
- 1 teaspoon ground black pepper
- ¼ - ½ teaspoon cayenne
- 1 shallot (minced)
- 2 garlic cloves (minced)
- Salt to taste
- chives (garnish)
- carrot chips (garnish)

Carrot chips:

- 2-3 thick, medium-large carrots
- salt to taste

Method:

For the carrot chips:

1. Start by preheating your oven to 225° F.
2. You want to use thick (meaning having a large diameter) carrots for the chips because they shrink up a lot during the dehydration process. Slice carrots very thinly into rounds using a mandoline or a very sharp knife.
3. Place carrots on a rack fitted over a baking sheet in a single layer. Sprinkle lightly with salt and bake for an hour to an hour and 15 minutes. They should be relatively

crispy at that point, but will crisp even more as they cool. Cool completely before serving.

For the tartare:

1. Bring a medium pot of water up to a boil and season heavily with salt. While the water is coming up, prepare an ice bath (a bowl of cold water with ice). You want to cook the carrots and then shock them in the ice bath to stop the cooking.

2. When the water comes up to a boil, add the carrots and cook until a fork slips easily into the thickest part of the carrot. That can vary depending on the width — I would say anywhere from 6 to 12 minutes. Transfer immediately to the ice water to stop the cooking. Remove and dry thoroughly. At this point, you can move ahead or save them in the refrigerator for use a day or two later.

3. If you have a stand mixer with a meat grinder attachment, pass the cooled and dry carrots through the larger, coarse grinding plate. If not, you can use a ricer or a food processor to achieve a ground carrot texture. You don't want mush, so try not to take it too far!

4. Heat the butter in a medium saucepan over medium heat. Add spices and toast for a minute or so until fragrant and nutty. The butter should brown a bit. Add the shallot and garlic and cook another 30 seconds to a minute. Toss in the ground carrots until they are heated through. They should be warm and touchable.

5. Serve warm (you can use a ring mold if you like) and top with chopped chives and carrot chips, if using.

Beg Wot (Ethiopian Lamb Stew)

Serves: 4

Ingredients:

- 1-1 ½ kg lamb
- 750 g onion
- 125 ml olive oil
- 2 cloves of garlic
- 2 cm piece of ginger (about same amount as garlic)
- 2 tablespoons berbere
- 1 teaspoon salt
- ½ teaspoon black pepper
- 1 can (400g) tomato (optional, see note)

Method:

1. First, chop the onion finely (in a food processor).
2. Bring water (about 750ml) to a boil.
3. Add the onion to a large pot and cook. Cover the onion with a lid and stir regularly ensuring that the onion does not burn.
4. Only when necessary add a little water to stop the onion from burning.
5. When the onion is soft and translucent add the oil (after about 10-15 minutes).
6. Cook 10 minutes until golden. (Optional – see note: add 1 tablespoon tomato puree)
7. Add the berbere and cook on the lowest heat for about 30 minutes stirring once in a while. Only when the onions begin to stick, add a few drops of water.
8. Add the canned tomato.
9. Cut the meat into small bite size pieces.

10. Add the lam to the onion.
11. Press garlic and ginger through a garlic press into the pot.
12. Cook the meat, stirring regularly until the meat is just cooked. They say the sauce is done when oil rises to surface. (Depending on the meat this takes about 10 -30 minutes.) When the sauce thickens (after about 10 minutes) add about 200ml-500ml boiling water. You are looking for a thick and glossy stew.
13. Season with salt and pepper.
14. Serve with Injera bread.

Note:

- Instead of using the can of tomatoes you can add 1 tablespoon of tomato puree before adding the berbere.

Ethiopian-Style Beef Stir Fry

Serves: 1

Ingredients:

- 1 ½ pounds hanger steak or beef tenderloin (cut into 1/2-inch cubes)
- 6 thin slices navel orange (quartered)
- 3 medium-large ripe tomatoes (chopped) or 1 ½ cups drained, roughly chopped canned tomatoes
- 3 cloves garlic (quartered)
- 2 jalapeños (seeded and thinly sliced)
- 2 red onions (sliced)
- 1 bunch broccolini (in 2-inch pieces)
- 1 tablespoon mild chili powder
- ½ cup unsalted dry-roasted peanuts (coarsely chopped)
- ½ cup dry red wine
- ½ teaspoon ground cardamom
- ½ teaspoon ground ginger
- ¼ teaspoon freshly ground black pepper
- ¼ cup peanut oil
- salt to taste

Method:

1. Start by mixing the chili powder, cardamom, ginger, and pepper in a bowl. Add the beef and toss to coat.
2. Heat the oil in a large skillet on medium-high heat. Add the onions and garlic and sauté, stirring constantly, until they begin to brown on the edges. Add the meat, sprinkle it with 1 teaspoon salt, and stir-fry until it is browned on all sides.

3. Reduce the heat and add the tomatoes, broccolini, jalapeños, peanuts, and wine. Simmer for about a minute, then season with salt if needed. Cook for about 2 minutes more.
4. Serve, garnished with orange pieces.

Ethiopian Beef Tibs

Serves: 2-3

Ingredients:

- 1-pound beef sirloin (cut into 1-inch cubes, trimmed of excess fat and connective tissue)
- 6 medium cloves garlic (minced)
- 5 tablespoons niter kibbeh (or plain unsalted butter)
- 3-inch knob ginger (minced)
- 2 tablespoons berbere
- 2 medium-large onions (chopped medium)
- 1 teaspoon vegetable oil
- 1 teaspoon lemon juice to taste
- kosher salt

Method:

1. First, melt niter kibbeh or butter in a heavy saucepan on medium heat, then add onions, ginger, garlic, and berbere. Reduce heat to medium-low and cook, stirring occasionally, until onions are dark, ruddy, and golden, about 30 minutes. Onions should be at a low sizzle during cooking process. Adjust heat accordingly.
2. Transfer to food processor and blend until not quite a purée. Return to saucepan, season to taste with salt, and keep warm.
3. Season beef on all sides generously with kosher salt. Heat oil in a 12-inch cast iron or stainless-steel skillet over high heat high until lightly smoking. Add beef in a single layer, leaving plenty of open space in the pan (brown in batches if you don't have a large enough skillet).

4. Cook without moving until well-seared on one side, about 3 minutes. Flip meat cubes with tongs and cook on second side until well seared. Continue to cook meat, stirring and flipping occasionally until desired level of doneness is reached.
5. For rare meat, transfer to saucepan immediately. For medium, cook an additional one to two minutes before transferring to saucepan. For well done, cook up to five more minutes before transferring to saucepan.
6. Toss beef with warm sauce, stir in lemon juice, and serve immediately.

Ye'abesha Gomen (Ethiopian Collard Greens)

Serves: 4

Ingredients:

- 10-ounce Collard Greens/Kale (chopped)
- 3 or more tablespoons Niter Ethiopian Spiced Butter or cooking oil
- 2 teaspoon garlic (minced)
- 1-2 fresh chili pepper or ½ teaspoon cayenne pepper or more
- 1 ½ teaspoon ginger (minced)
- 1 large white onion (chopped)
- 1 teaspoon smoke paprika
- 1 teaspoon coriander/cumin
- 1 fresh lemon
- ½ teaspoon cardamom spice

Method:

1. In a large skillet, add oil, spiced butter, garlic, ginger, chili pepper, cumin, cardamom, paprika, sauté for about 30 seconds or more, be careful not to let the ingredients burn.
2. Then add onions, mix with the spices. Sauté for about 3-5
3. Throw in chopped collards, cayenne pepper, lemon juice, continue cooking for another 7-10 minutes until flavors have blend and greens are cooked, according to preference. Adjust seasonings –Salt and pepper, turn off the heat.
4. Remove from the heat and let it cool.
5. Serve with Injera.

Ethiopian Atakilt Wat with Lentils and Toasted Naan

Serves: 2

Ingredients:

- 1 lb. yellow potatoes
- 3 medium carrots (loose)
- 3 tablespoons extra virgin olive oil
- 3 cups water
- 3 cloves garlic
- 2 cups green cabbage
- 2 pieces naan
- 1 ½ teaspoon berbere spice
- 1 lime
- 1 yellow onions
- ½-inch piece ginger
- ¾ cup green lentils
- salt and pepper to taste

Method:

Prepare the Ingredients:

1. Dice the onion. Mince the garlic and ginger.
2. Rinse the lentils in a fine sieve. Cut the lime in half.
3. Rinse the carrots and cut them into ¼-inch thick coins.
4. Rinse and scrub the potatoes, and cut them into ½-inch cubes.
5. Rinse and dice the cabbage.

Make the Atakilt Wat:

1. Heat 2 tablespoons olive oil in a large pot over medium heat.

2. Add the onion, garlic, ginger and Ethiopian spice mix, and cook until tender and fragrant, about 2-3 minutes.
3. Stir in the carrots, potatoes, cabbage, 1 cup of water and salt and pepper to taste.
4. Bring to simmer and cook for 10 minutes, stirring halfway through.
5. Add the lentils and 2 cups of water. Continue to simmer until the lentils and potatoes are tender, about another 15 minutes, stirring halfway through.

Toast the Naan:

1. When the Atakilt Wat is almost ready, heat 1 tbsp. olive oil in a large pan over medium heat.
2. Add a piece of naan and cook until toasted, about 1 minute per side. Repeat with the second piece of naan.
3. Cut the naan into wedges, if desired.

Bring It All Together:

1. Evenly divide the Atakilt Wat between two bowls.
2. Squeeze the lime juice on top and serve with toasted naan.

Kik Alicha (Ethiopian Dal)

Serves: 2-3

Ingredients:

- 6 cups vegetable broth
- 6 garlic cloves (minced)
- 2 cups dried yellow split peas
- 2 small onions (diced)
- 1 teaspoon turmeric
- ½ - 1 teaspoon *berbere spice* (or to taste)
- ½ teaspoon mild curry powder
- ½ teaspoon ground ginger
- ½ teaspoon garam masala
- salt and pepper to taste

Method:

1. In a pot, bring the 6 cups veggie broth to a boil and add the split peas, then cover and reduce heat to low. Simmer for 30 minutes.
2. While the split peas are simmering, sauté onions and garlic in a nonstick skillet until onions are translucent. Add spices and thoroughly mix to coat the onion.
3. Add onion mixture to split peas and simmer for 5 minutes, stirring and scraping the peas to keep them from sticking to the bottom of the pan.
4. Taste and add another ⅛ - ¼ tsp Berbere' if desired. Salt and pepper to taste.

Gored Gored (Ethiopian Seasoned Cubed Meat)

Serves: 10

Ingredients:

- 4 tablespoon neter kiba (seasoned butter)
- 4 tablespoon berbere awaze
- 2 pounds of tender beef

Method:

1. Cut the beef in cubes and on a medium skillet melt the butter (Kibe) at low heat.
2. Mix the beef and berbere Awaze in the butter.
3. Sautee at high heat for 1-3 minutes continuously stirring until the meat cooked rare, medium or well done depending on your taste.
4. Traditionally, it is served rare. Add a pinch of salt to taste and enjoy with injera or rice.

Asa Be Mitmita (Ethiopian Fried Fish with Mitmita)

Serves: 2-3

Ingredients:

- white fillet fish
- 2 teaspoons of Mitmita (You could use chilli powder as an alternative)
- 8 teaspoons of white plain flour
- ½ cup of fine breadcrumbs
- 1 teaspoon of turmeric
- 1 medium egg
- cooking oil
- salt and pepper (to taste)

Method:

1. Mix the flour and Mitmita, salt and pepper together and set aside.
2. Beat one egg and set aside.
3. Mix the breadcrumbs with the Turmeric and set aside.
4. Now that you have 3 separate items simply, coat the fish in the flour then the egg then the breadcrumbs.
5. Make sure at all 3 stages a good coating is made to your fish.
6. Heat 2cm of cooking oil (you can use corn or sunflower if you like) in a skillet.
7. Now place the breaded fish in the oil and cook for 4 mins on each side or until a deep golden brown.
8. Now place the fish on paper towels to remove any oil and serve.

Note:

- You can use any type of fish you want, including whole fish with bones. But adjust your cooking time.

Chapter Three: Ethiopian Dinner Recipes

Doro Wot (Ethiopian Chicken Stew)

Serves: 4-6

Ingredients:

- 2 lbs. (800g) of chicken thighs and drumsticks
- 11 ounces (450mls) of water or chicken stock (add as required)
- 6 tablespoons vegetable oil or niter kibbeh (fragrant butter)
- 6 teaspoons berbere spice mix or less, depending on what sort of heat you can take
- 6 medium-large red onions
- 6 medium eggs
- 2-3 garlic cloves
- 1 tablespoon garam masala
- 1 inch of fresh ginger
- 1 lemon (juiced)
- salt and pepper to taste

Method:

1. First, marinate the chicken pieces in the lemon juice.
2. In the meantime, finely chop the onions, garlic, and ginger by hand or blend into a paste in a food processor or hand-held chopper.
3. To make doro wat in its most authentic form, add the onions to a thick-bottomed pan and cook gently for an hour until the onions have cooked and reduced into a sweet paste.

4. Add the niter kibbeh, or vegetable oil. Olive oil is not typically used, as this has a strong flavor which may take away from the authentic spices used in doro wat. Add the berbere spice, followed by the ginger and garlic and fry until fragrant.
5. More berbere spice can be added depending on how much heat is desired from the dish.
6. Add the chicken pieces into the pan. Simmer on a low heat for 40 minutes until the chicken is cooked. Halfway through, sprinkle the garam masala over the wat. You may need to top up with a little water as required and stir occasionally to avoid sticking to the base of the pan.
7. While this is simmering away, boil your eggs.
8. After 40 minutes of simmering, add the boiled, shelled eggs to the wat. Serve the doro wat on top of injera to enjoy it the traditional way.

Ethiopian Lentil Stew - Vegan

Serves: 4

Ingredients:

- 1 cup dry lentils (soaked for 2 hours)
- 2 cups or more broth vegetable/chicken or water
- 2 tablespoons or more chopped parsley/cilantro
- 2 teaspoons garlic (minced)
- 1 ½ tablespoons berbere spice
- 1-2 tablespoons spiced butter
- 1-2 teaspoons smoked paprika
- 1 teaspoon coriander or cumin
- 1 tablespoons tomato paste
- 1 medium-large onion (diced)
- ½ tablespoon fresh ginger (minced)
- ¼ cup cooking oil
- salt and pepper to taste

Method:

1. Heat up large sauce-pan with oil, spiced butter, then add onions, berbere spice, garlic, ginger, cumin, and smoked paprika, stir occasionally for about 2-3 minutes until onions is translucent.
2. Then add soaked lentils, tomato paste, stir and sauté for about 2-3 more minutes.
3. Add stock / water if necessary, to prevent any burns. Salt to taste.
4. Bring to a boil and let it simmer until sauce thickens, it might take about 30 minutes or depending on how you like your lentils. Throw in some parsley, adjust for salt, pepper and stew consistency.

5. Serve warm.

Ethiopian Berbere Spiced Chickpeas Over Polenta

Serves: 4

Ingredients:

- 1-14 oz. can or 1 ¾ cups cooked chickpeas (rinsed and drained)
- 1 roll 18 oz. precooked polenta (cut into 1-inch slabs)
- 3 garlic cloves (minced)
- 2 teaspoons fresh ginger (grated)
- 2 teaspoons sugar
- 2 teaspoons berbere seasoning
- 1 ½ tablespoons olive oil (divided)
- 1 cup vegetable broth
- 1 medium-large green bell pepper (diced)
- ½ red onion (diced)
- ¼ cup tomato paste
- ¼ teaspoons salt
- ¼ cup fresh cilantro (chopped)

Method:

Prepare the Polenta:

1. First, coat a large skillet with ½ tablespoon of olive oil and place over medium-high heat.
2. Arrange polenta slabs in a single layer and cook about 5 minutes, until bottoms become crispy and begin to brown.
3. Gently flip and repeat on other side. Do this in batches if you don't have enough room.
4. Transfer polenta slabs to a plate and set aside.

Prepare the Chickpeas:

1. Heat remaining 1 tablespoon of olive oil in a large skillet over medium heat. Add onion and sauté until softened, about 5 minutes.
2. Add garlic and ginger. Sauté for another minute.
3. Add broth, chickpeas, tomato paste, sugar, berbere seasoning, and salt. Lower heat and simmer for 5 minutes.
4. Add bell pepper and simmer another 5 minutes, until pepper is softened and sauce is thick. Add a bit of water if sauce becomes too thick during cooking.

Serve:

1. Arrange polenta slabs on plates and top with chickpeas. Sprinkle with cilantro.

Misr Wat (Spicy Ethiopian Red Lentils)

Serves: 4

Ingredients:

- 1 cup red lentils (rinsed)
- 4 cloves garlic (minced)
- 4 tablespoons extra virgin olive oil
- 2 tablespoons berbere
- 2 cups water
- 1 lime (juiced)
- 1 medium-large red onion (diced)
- 1 teaspoon fresh ginger (grated)
- ½ - 1 teaspoon kosher salt
- 2 tablespoons chopped cilantro (optional)

Method:

1. Prepare a medium size pot to boil the water. Add the lentils and cook according to the package directions, though leave them a little al dente, as they will simmer in a spiced liquid a little later in the recipe. About 5 -10 minutes, depending on the size of the lentils. Drain the lentils and set aside.

2. Warm the olive oil in a large sauté pan, over medium heat. Add the onion and cook until softened, about 5 minutes. Add the garlic and ginger, cook for 2 minutes. Stir in the berbere to form a paste.

3. Add the lentils, ½ teaspoon of salt, and water. Bring to a simmer for 10 - 15 minutes, until most of the water has evaporated and the mixture has thickened into a stew-like consistency. Taste and add more salt, if need. Finish with fresh lime juice.

4. Garnish with cilantro (if desired) and serve immediately. Enjoy!

Note:

- If you prefer something a little milder, start with 1 tablespoon of the berbere spice mix.

Ethiopian Meal

Serves: 4-6

Ingredients:

Injera starter:

- ¾ cup water at 70° (plus 1 cup, divided)
- ½ cup teff flour (plus 2/3 cup, divided)
- 1/8 teaspoon dry active yeast

Injera:

- 1 ¾ cups water at room temperature
- 1 ¾ cups teff flour
- ¼ cup starter from above
- generous pinch of sea salt
- vegetable oil (for greasing)

Braised cabbage:

- 3 tablespoons olive oil
- 2 medium-large carrots (peeled and diced)
- 1 medium-large cabbage head (cut into 8 wedges)
- 1 large onion (peeled and sliced)
- 1 teaspoon freshly ground cumin
- salt and pepper to taste
- pinch red pepper flakes (optional)
- 1 teaspoon turmeric (optional)

Mustard lentils:

- 1 cup puy lentils (or other lentils, such as green or black)
- 1 teaspoon black mustard seeds

- ½ teaspoon black peppercorns
- 1 teaspoon sea salt
- pinch of cayenne pepper
- 1 large lemon (juiced)
- 3 tablespoons olive oil
- 1 chili or jalapeño (seeded and minced)

Method:

Make the starter:

1. Start by whisking all the ingredients in a bowl or a glass jar, cover with something breathable like cheesecloth and leave to rest at room temperature for 2 days. You should see some rising along the way.
2. Stir the starter. It will smell very grassy, almost in a spoiled kind of way (it might even make you think that it went bad—it likely did not). Resist the urge to throw it away; the smell indicates fermentation, and that's what we're looking for. You also should see bubbles on the surface. Feed the starter with 1/3 cup teff flour and ½ cup water, cover and leave to ferment for another 2 days.
3. The starter may separate into 2 layers at this point— that's fine. Stir it and feed with another 1/3 cup teff flour and ½ cup water. Cover and let ferment for at least another 4 hours or overnight.
4. After that, your starter is ready.

Make the injera:

1. In a large bowl, dissolve the starter in water. Add in the flour and whisk into a smooth pancake batter. Cover and let ferment for 5 to 6 hours. Reserve 1/4 cup of starter for the next batch, if desired.

2. Add in salt, whisk again to dissolve and begin cooking the injera. Optionally, you can add 1/2 teaspoon of baking soda to get more bubbles.
3. Heat a non-stick pan or skillet with a tight-fitting lid over medium heat. Lightly grease it with vegetable oil using a paper towel.
4. Add about 1/3 to 1/2 cup of batter to the pan, depending on its size, tilting and swirling to cover the surface evenly. Cook for about 1 minute, until bubbles appear on the surface.
5. Cover with a lid and steam the injera for about 3 minutes, until the top is set and the bread easily pulls off the pan. No need to flip it over. Remove it and continue with the rest of the batter. It will take a few tries to get the temperature and the cooking time just right.

Make the braised cabbage:

1. Preheat oven to 325°. Snugly arrange the cabbage wedges, carrots and onion in a lightly oiled baking dish. Drizzle olive oil and broth/water over it, followed by salt, cumin, pepper and turmeric, if using.
2. Cover with foil and braise for 1 hour. Remove the dish from the oven and carefully flip the cabbage, carrots and onion. Braise for another hour. Increase oven temperature to 400°.
3. Remove the foil and place the dish back into the oven for another 15-20 minutes, until the vegetables are golden brown.

Make the mustard lentils:

1. Cook the lentils in plenty of salted water until soft, 15 minutes or so, depending on the type of lentils.

2. Grind the mustard seeds and peppercorns with a mortar and pestle. Add in the salt and cayenne and pour 1 tablespoon of boiling water over the spices. Add lemon juice and olive oil and stir to combine.
3. Add the chili or jalapeño into the lentils and pour the dressing over them. Toss well to combine. Adjust salt to taste.
4. Serve with braised cabbage and lentil salad with warm injera for scooping.

Doro Tibs Wat (Spicy Ethiopian Chicken)

Serves: 2

Ingredients:

- ½-pound chicken breast (cubed)
- 2 teaspoons mitmita (Ethiopian chili powder) or cayenne pepper
- 1 teaspoon fresh garlic (chopped)
- 1 teaspoon fresh ginger (chopped)
- ½ fresh tomato, diced, or 1 tablespoon tomato paste (optional, to reduce the spiciness)
- ½ medium spanish onion (peeled and chopped)
- ¼ cup vegetable oil
- ¼ teaspoon ground cumin
- ¼ teaspoon ground cardamom
- salt and pepper to taste

Method:

1. In a skillet over low heat, combine the oil, onion, garlic, ginger, chili powder, cumin and cardamom, and cook, stirring, for 30 minutes.
2. If you have a low tolerance for spice, add tomato.
3. Then add the chicken and cook about 10 minutes, until the meat is cooked through.
4. Finally, add salt and pepper to taste.
5. Serve with injera bread or white rice.

Awaze Tibs (Ethiopian Lamb & Onion Stew)

Serves: 2-3

Ingredients:

- 1.2 lbs. lamb (cubed)
- 3 cloves garlic (crushed)
- 2 teaspoons berbere spice
- 2 red onions (chopped)
- 1-inch ginger root (freshly peeled & grated, about 1 ½ teaspoon)
- 1 cup beef broth
- 1/8 cup peanut oil
- plain yogurt to taste
- salt and pepper to taste

Method:

1. First, chop the onions and cook them until golden, about 10-15 minutes, over medium high.
2. Meanwhile, grate the ginger and add with fresh garlic to the pan and cook a few more minutes.
3. Add berbere spice and the meat and brown it.
4. Cover with beef stock and simmer partially covered for about 35 minutes, or until the lamb is tender. (If you'd like a less soupy texture simmer uncovered).
5. Season with salt and pepper.

Berbere Chicken with Ethiopian Lentils

Serves: 6

Ingredients:

Chicken:

- 6 medium chicken thighs (skin-on)
- 2-3 tablespoons berbere spice
- olive oil
- kosher Salt

For the meatball curry:

- 5 cloves garlic (minced)
- 3 cups water
- 2-3 tablespoons *berbere spice*
- 2 cups onions (diced)
- 2 tablespoon olive oil
- 1 tablespoon fresh ginger (minced)
- 1 cup carrot (diced)
- 1 cup French Green (Indigo or Beluga Caviar lentils, do not use a split lentil)
- 1 cup tomato (diced)
- 1 teaspoon salt
- fresh Italian parsley for garnish

Method:

1. Start by preheating your oven to 400 F.
2. In a heavy bottom pot, or dutch oven, sauté diced onion, carrots, garlic and ginger in 2 tablespoons olive oil, until tender, about 5-7 minutes. Add 2-3 tablespoons Berbere Spice mix and sauté for about 2-3 minutes. Add 1 cup

lentils, 1 cup diced tomatoes, 1 teaspoon salt and 3 cups water, bring to a boil, cover, turn heat to low and let cook until al dente, about 30 minutes.

3. Pat Dry Chicken and salt all sides with salt and pepper.
4. Generously rub each piece with some berbere spice.
5. Heat 1 tablespoon oil in a heavy bottom pan/skillet, on medium-high heat, place chicken skin side down and sear until it is crispy and golden, about 6-8 minutes. Turn over, and turn heat down to medium, searing for about 2-3 minutes. Place in a 400 F oven until internal temperature reaches 165F (10-15 minutes)
6. Serve over a bed of the Ethiopian lentils, and garnish with fresh Italian parsley.

Berbere spice:

1. If using whole seeds, lightly toast them on the stove top in a skillet for 2-3 minutes.
2. Grind them using a coffee grinder or mortar and pestle. Remember to crush or grind the chili flakes.
3. Enjoy with rice, vegetable curries, lentils or fried rice.

Beef Kitfo (Ethiopian Tartare) with Injera Crisps

Serves: 4-6

Ingredients:

For the Injera crisps:

- 2 to 4 pieces injera (roughly torn into 4-inch pieces)

For the spiced butter:

- 4 garlic cloves (halved)
- 3-inch piece ginger (peeled and sliced)
- 1 jalapeño (halved)
- 1 tablespoon *berbere spice*
- ½ cup unsalted butter

For the Kitfo:

- 1-pound strip loin (trimmed and diced into ¼-inch pieces)
- 2 cured anchovy fillets (finely diced)
- 2 shallots (finely diced)
- 2 tablespoons fresh lemon juice (from 1 lemon)
- 1¼ teaspoons kosher salt (plus more to taste)
- 1 lemon (zested using a vegetable peeler and white pith removed)
- 1 small gala apple (diced)
- 1 tablespoon Dijon mustard
- 1 tablespoon *berbere spice*
- ¼ teaspoon freshly ground black pepper
- ¼ cup unsalted butter

Method:

Make the injera crisps:

1. Start by preheating the oven to 325° and line a sheet tray with parchment paper. Place the injera in a single layer on the prepared baking sheet and bake until crisp, about 15 to 17 minutes.

Make the spiced butter:

1. In a large sauté pan, combine the spiced butter ingredients and place over low heat, slowly melting and infusing the butter for 15 minutes. Remove from the heat and set aside.

Make the Kitfo:

1. In a separate large sauté pan, melt the butter with the lemon zest over medium heat. When the butter begins to foam, add the shallots and cook until translucent, 10 to 12 minutes. Add the apple, lemon juice, mustard and berbere, stirring to mix together, and cook 1 minute more. Remove from the heat and keep warm.
2. Strain the spiced butter into a large bowl and discard the solids. Reserve the sauté pan as is, without wiping clean, and return to medium-high heat. Place the beef in a large bowl and season with the salt and pepper. Add half of the beef mixture and cook, stirring occasionally, for 30 seconds. Add 2 to 4 tablespoons of the spiced butter and cook 30 seconds more, then remove from the heat and pour back into the remaining raw beef mixture. Fold in the apple-shallot mixture and anchovies, and stir just until combined. Adjust the seasoning to taste with salt. Don't overmix.

3. To serve, place a few pieces of injera crisps on a plate and top with the kitfo.

Yetakelt W'et (Ethiopian Vegetable Stew with Braised Tempeh)

Serves: 2

Ingredients:

- 1 cake tempeh* (cubed)
- 6 cloves garlic (minced)
- 2 tablespoons parsley (minced)
- 2 tablespoons scallion (minced)
- 2 tablespoons olive oil
- 2 red potatoes (diced)
- 1 ½ tablespoon *berbere spice*
- 1 ½ -2 cups vegetable stock or water
- 1 medium-large carrot (chunked)
- 1 handful green beans
- 1 cup mushrooms (chopped)
- 1 large red onion (chopped)
- 1 tablespoon smoked paprika
- 1 medium-large tomato (chopped)
- ¼ cup tomato paste
- ¼ cup coconut oil
- salt to taste

Method:

1. Start by roasting all the vegetables. You can braise the tempeh simultaneously.
2. Heat the oven to 450 F. Put all the vegetables, sans tomato, with the olive oil, some salt, and 2 cloves of garlic. Spread on a pizza or baking pan, put a rack at oven bottom, and oven for about 15 minutes, tossing every 5

minutes. Add a little water after the first and second tosses, to steam the taters.

3. Put the tempeh with a little sesame or coconut oil, some salt or bragg's, black pepper and 1 clove of the garlic. And a dash of berbere spice.

4. Set the tempeh in a baking dish in a single layer, add enough water (or vegetables stock) to just barely cover the tempeh, and put it in the oven with the vegetables. You want to give it at least 15 minutes to steam/braise, to get rid of the bitter taste tempeh often has. Ideally, all your liquid will be gone - but it isn't necessary.

5. Heat your coconut oil in a deep pot and add onion and garlic. Sauté for about 2 minutes. Add berbere and paprika, toss and toast a bit. Add your tomatoes and paste - stir and cook about 4-5 minutes, until the fresh maters have softened.

6. Scrape the entire baking pan of vegetables into your pot, and add a cup of stock. Add your tempeh. You want a thick stew, but some sauce to sop with injera - add stock until the consistency is reached.

7. Stir in your salt, parsley and scallion.

8. Serve.

Ethiopian Spicy Fish Stew with Red Onion

Serves: 4-6

Ingredients:

- 2 lbs. fish
- 3-4 cups medium red onions (chopped)
- ½ cup vegetable or peanut oil
- ½ cup dry red wine or T'ej (Ethiopian wine)
- ¼ cup berbere spice (more if desired)
- ¼ teaspoon ground black pepper

Method:

1. First, cut fish into serving sized pieces, arrange on broiler pan and brush with oil. Broil until cooked through, then keep warm. You can also cook the fish through on a grill.
2. Heat a large, heavy skillet or pan. When it is hot, add the onions all at once to the dry pan.
3. Let the onions cook on medium heat, stirring frequently to keep them from sticking. If they stick, you can add a little bit of water. After about 15 minutes, the onions should be soft and beginning to brown.
4. Add oil, berbere spice and black pepper. Stir to combine with the onions.
5. Add wine and continue cooking and stirring until mixture comes to a boil.
6. Simmer on low heat (but keeping it at a boil) for at least 30 minutes, until sauce is thickened and favors are married together.
7. Add fish fillets to pan. Stir gently to combine with the sauce.
8. Serve hot with injera.

Berbere Spiced Chicken Breasts

Serves: 1

Ingredients:

- 1 skinless, boneless chicken breast half (lightly pounded to an even thickness)
- 2 teaspoons butter
- 2 teaspoons tomato paste
- 1 tablespoon chopped cilantro
- 1 teaspoon kosher salt
- 1 tablespoon berbere spice blend (or to taste)
- 1 lime (juiced)
- ½ teaspoon *berbere spice* (or to taste)
- 1/3 cup coconut milk
- ¼ cup chicken broth (or as needed)
- salt to taste

Method:

1. Start by seasoning both sides of chicken breast with salt. Sprinkle 1 tablespoon berbere spice mix to coat both sides of chicken breast.
2. In a skillet or pan, melt butter over medium-high heat until it just starts to turn brown. Transfer chicken breast immediately to skillet; cook about 2 to 3 minutes per side. Transfer chicken to a warm dish.
3. Stir in lime juice, tomato paste, chicken broth, and coconut milk; stir to deglaze pan. Bring to a simmer while stirring. Add 1/2 teaspoon berbere spice and a pinch of salt. Transfer chicken breast back to skillet; reduce heat to medium-low. Cook until chicken is cooked through and sauce starts to reduce, basting chicken with pan

juices as it cooks, 4 or 5 more minutes. An instant-read thermometer inserted into the center should read at least 165 degrees F (74 degrees C).

4. Sprinkle with chopped cilantro. Serve with a drizzle of the pan sauce.

Sega Wat (Spicy Ethiopian Beef Stew)

Serves: 6

Ingredients:

- 2 pounds boneless beef chuck (cut into ½-inch cubes)
- 6 tablespoons niter kibbeh (divided)
- 4 hard-boiled eggs (shelled and pierced all over with a fork ¼ inch deep)
- 3 cups chunky pureed onions (pulse in food processor to form a chunky paste)
- 1 ½ tablespoons garlic (minced)
- 1 ½ tablespoons fresh ginger (minced)
- 1 ½ teaspoons salt
- 1 cup strong beef broth
- ¼ cup berbere spice

Method:

1. Start by heating 3 tablespoons of niter kibbeh or butter in a heavy pot or Dutch oven. Add the onions and cook, covered, over low heat for 20 minutes, stirring occasionally.
2. Add the garlic, ginger, and 1 tablespoon niter kibbeh and continue to cook for another 10 minutes, stirring occasionally.
3. Add the berbere and the 2 remaining tablespoons of niter kibbeh and cook, covered, over low heat for another 10 minutes, stirring occasionally.
4. Add the beef, broth, salt and bring to a boil. Reduce the heat to low, cover, and simmer for 45 minutes, stirring occasionally.

5. Adjust the seasonings, adding more berbere according to taste and heat preference. Add the hard-boiled eggs and simmer on low heat, covered, for another 10 to heat through.
6. Half or quarter the eggs and arrange on the plates with the stew.
7. Serve hot with Ethiopian injera, bread or rice.

Zizil Alicha Wot (Ethiopian Beef Stew)

Serves: 2-3

Ingredients:

- 300-gram lean beef (cut into 2 or 3 long strips)
- 3 tablespoons butter
- 3 cloves of garlic (chopped finely)
- 2 jalapeno chilies (cut into long strips)
- 1 clove (ground)
- 1 white or red onion
- 1 teaspoon turmeric
- ¼ teaspoon cinnamon
- olive or sunflower oil
- a 2.5 cm / 1-inch piece of fresh ginger (grated or chopped)
- pinch of nutmeg
- content of one cardamom pod (ground)
- salt to taste

Method:

1. Start by heating the oil in a pan or skillet with a non-stick surface, add the meat and fry it for about 8 to 10 minutes.
2. Add 2 tablespoons of butter, lower the heat to medium and continue to fry the meat for another one or two minutes till it becomes a little crispy.
3. Remove the meat from the pan and keep it warm in the oven.
4. Leave the oil in the pan to use for the gravy. Add the onions to the pan and cook them till they are golden brown. This should take about 5 to 6 minutes.

5. Add the Turmeric, garlic, ginger, cardamom, clove, cinnamon, salt and 100ml of water. Stir all and cover the pot letting the contents boil on low heat for 8 to 10 minutes.
6. Add another 100ml of water, stir content of pan, cover with the lid again and let it boil for another 15 minutes.
7. Once the meat is tender and the gravy has thickened a little add the green chilies, and let them simmer in the pot for another 3 to 4 minutes.
8. Serve hot with injera, potatoes or rice of your choice.

Wild Mushroom Stew with Spicy Berbere Sauce

Serves: 2-3

Ingredients:

- 500 gram / 17.6 oz garden mushrooms (or button mushrooms), chopped into squares or quartered depending on their sizes
- 4 cloves of garlic (finely chopped)
- 3 heaped teaspoons berbere spice
- 3 small onions (sliced)
- 3 small tomatoes (finely chopped)
- 2 green bell peppers (sliced)
- 2 handful spinach (roughly chopped)
- 1 tablespoon niter kibe for frying (or normal butter)

Method:

1. Start with adding niter kibe to a large frying pan and switch stove on to medium hot heat.
2. Fried potato, sweet potato and carrots.
3. Once the spicy butter is hot, add pepper, garlic, onions and tomatoes to the pan and mix well.
4. Fry for 5 minutes, stirring it frequently.
5. Add the berbere and mushrooms and carefully mix all ingredients.
6. Let it cook with a partially covered pan for 5 minutes or till the mushrooms are done.
7. Switch of heat, add the spinach and cover with the lid.
8. After 3 minutes take of the lid.
9. Serve with hot steamed rice, injera or fried potatoes, carrots and sweet potatoes.

Note:

- Please be very careful when picking wild mushrooms. Pick only those that you can identify with certainty to be suitable for consumption and stay away from any of those that you don't feel sure about. Mushrooms can be extremely poisonous!

Ethiopian Fried Chicken Wings

Serves: 2-3

Ingredients:

- 500 g chicken wings
- 3 teaspoons mitmita
- 3 cloves garlic
- 2 cm cube kibe
- 2 medium onion
- 2 teaspoons turmeric
- 1 cm cube ginger
- 1 cup plain flour
- cooking oil

Method:

1. Start by mixing the flour and turmeric tougher.
2. Now dust the wings in the flour mix, giving them a good coating.
3. Place them in the fridge for a min of 30 mins.
4. The chili butter – In a pan with a touch of oil add the onions, garlic and ginger.
5. Cook these for just about 3 mins. (It is important to chop all of this very small, we have used a food blender.)
6. Now add salt and pepper to taste along with the mitmita and cook with a lid on for 3 mins.
7. Add the kiddie and continue to cook for 2 mins. This is now done.
8. Remove the wings from the fridge and with around 1cm of hot oil fry the wings until golden brown, this should take around 6-7 mins.

9. Remove them and place of kitchen paper to remove any oil.
10. Simply now place the wings in a serving dish and pour over the hot butter mix.

Ye'difin Misser Alicha (Lentils in Garlic-Ginger Sauce Recipe) - Vegan Gluten-free Soy-free

Serves: 2

Ingredients:

- 1 cup dried green or brown lentils
- 6 cloves garlic (pressed or grated)
- 6 cups water
- 3 tablespoons extra-virgin olive oil
- 2 teaspoons fresh ginger (peeled and grated)
- 1 ½ cups reserved lentil cooking water (plus more if desired)
- 1-2 jalapeno chilis (seeded, veined, and sliced into thin half-moons)
- ½ cup onion (minced)
- ½ teaspoon salt (plus more if desired)
- ½ teaspoon ground turmeric
- 6 fresh basil leaves (optional)

Method:

1. Start by putting the lentils and water in a large saucepan and bring to a boil over high heat. Stir to keep the lentils from sticking to the bottom of the pot.
2. Decrease the heat to medium-high and simmer, skimming off and discarding any foam that forms with a large spoon. Cook uncovered, stirring occasionally, until the lentils are tender but still firm, 10 to 12 minutes.
3. Drain the lentils and reserve 2 cups of the cooking water.
4. While the lentils cook, put the onion, extra-virgin olive oil, and salt in a large saucepan and cook over medium

97

heat, stirring frequently, until soft and translucent (don't let the onion brown), about 7 minutes.

5. Add the garlic, ginger, optional basil, and turmeric and cook, stirring almost constantly, for 3 minutes.

6. Stir in the drained lentils and 1 ½ cups of the reserved cooking water. Increase the heat to high and bring to a boil. Decrease the heat to medium and simmer uncovered, stirring frequently, until the lentils are very soft but not mushy and the liquid has reduced and thickened, 10 to 15 minutes.

7. Add the jalapeno chiles during the last 5 minutes of cooking. If the mixture is too thick, add up to ½ cup additional lentil cooking water as needed to thin.

8. Season to taste with additional salt if desired.

9. Discard the basil before serving.

Yedoro Minchet Abish (Spicy Chicken Stew)

Serves: 1-2

Ingredients:

- 1-pound skinless boneless chicken meat (finely chopped)
- 3-4 tablespoons berbere spice (add or reduce to your taste)
- 4 tablespoons unsalted butter
- 2 cups onions (chopped)
- 1 ½ cups water
- ¾ cup red wine
- ½ teaspoon salt
- ½ teaspoon fresh ginger (minced)
- ½ teaspoon freshly ground black pepper
- 1/8 teaspoon green cardamom seed, ground, or ground cardamom

Method:

1. Cook the onions in a dry heavy saucepan over medium heat until lightly browned, stirring constantly to prevent burning. Add a dash of water if necessary if the onions are sticking to the pan.
2. Add the butter, spice paste, and salt, and cook over low heat for 15 minutes, stirring frequently. Add the wine and ginger, then add the chicken and cook over medium low heat for 10 minutes, or until the chicken has changed color.
3. Add the pepper, cardamom, and water, and bring to a gently boil, stirring occasionally. Lower the heat and

simmer for 10 to 15 minutes, uncovered, until the sauce has reduced and thickened.

4. Serve with injera, accompanied by green pepper relish and spiced curds.

Dullet (Spiced Tripe, Liver and Beef)

Serves: 2-3

Ingredients:

- 1 lb. lamb tripe
- 1 lb. lamb liver
- 1 lb. lean minced meat
- 2 medium chopped green pepper
- 1 tablespoon berbere
- 1 cup spiced butter
- ½ cup chopped red onions
- ½ teaspoon black pepper
- ½ teaspoon cardamom (koremina)
- salt to taste

Method:

1. Start by washing the liver and tripe over running water.
2. In a pan or a wok, cook onions along with the butter on a medium heat until softened.
3. Add all the spices and mix well.
4. Add all the meats, mix well. Cook for about 10-15 minutes or until all the meat turns golden brown.
5. Serve while hot.

Ye Qwant'a Zilbo (Dried Beef Stew)

Serves: 2-3

Ingredients:

- 1 lb. dried beef
- 2 ½ cups water
- 2 cups chopped red onions
- 1 cup niter kibbeh
- 1 cup shiro water
- ½ cup *berbere spice*
- ¼ teaspoon ground fenugreek

Method:

1. In a medium pan or wok, fry onions until brown, add fenugreek and stir well.
2. Little by little, add 1 cup water.
3. Add berbere and kibosh, stirring well.
4. In another pan on a medium heat add the beef and 2 cups of water.
5. Cook until beef is soft.
6. Once soft remove beef from water and add to the onion mix.
7. In a bowl dissolve shiro in water, allow to the shiro to rest on the bottom of the bowl about 5 minutes.
8. Add the shiro water to the beef and onion mixture.
9. Simmer for 30 minutes.
10. Serve with Ethiopian Injera.

Missir Wot Pizza - Vegan

Serves: 2-3

Ingredients:

Crust:

- 2 tablespoons tapioca starch
- 2 tablespoons potato starch
- 2 teaspoons raw sugar
- 2 teaspoon extra virgin olive oil
- 1 teaspoon active yeast
- ½ teaspoon apple cider vinegar
- 1/3 cup water
- ¼ cup teff flour
- ¼ cup oat flour
- ¼ teaspoon salt
- 1/8 teaspoon baking powder
- a generous pinch of cumin powder (optional)

Missir wot (whole red lentil stew):

- 4-5 garlic cloves
- 2 cups water
- 2 teaspoons extra virgin olive oil
- 2 teaspoons berbere spice
- ½ cup whole lentils sabut masoor, brown lentils soaked for atleast 2 hours to overnight
- ½ medium-large onion (chopped)
- 1/3 teaspoon salt

Toppings:

- chopped kale or other greens

- shredded vegan cheese
- chopped cilantro or fresh herbs of choice

Method:

Miss wot (whole red lentil stew):

1. Add oil in a pressure cooker or pan and heat over low-medium.
2. Add the onion and garlic and cook until translucent. 10-12 minutes.
3. Add the berbere spice and mix. cook for a minute.
4. Add the soaked lentils, salt and water. Mix well and cook over medium for 2 whistles in whistling pressure cooker then on low for 15 minutes. (10 minutes after the pressure has reached for electric pressure cooker)
5. If using pan, add them to the onion mixture along with salt, water and cook on medium, partially covered until the lentils start to disintegrate. 40-45 minutes.
6. Taste and adjust salt and spice, take off heat and keep ready.
7. You can also use pink/red lentils for a quicker cooking time.

Crust:

1. Add warm water, yeast and sugar in a bowl, mix well and let sit for 10 minutes or until frothy.
2. In another bowl, mix all the flours, starches, salt, baking powder and spice/cumin if using.
3. Add dry flours to yeast mixture. Add extra virgin olive oil and vinegar and whisk into a smooth batter.
4. Let the batter sit for 1 ½ hours. The batter with rise and becomes spongy.
5. Mix it and drop onto parchment lined sheet.

6. Drizzle a teaspoon of extra virgin olive oil and 'lightly' pat down the batter into desired shape using your hands. Spray water liberally on top.
7. You can also make the crust in an 8-inch cake pan to make a slightly fatter and even softer crust.

Making the pizza:

1. Preheat the oven to 375º F / 190º C. and let the crust sit near the oven or in a warm place for 10 to 15 minutes. you should see that the crust rises a bit.
2. Bake in preheated 375º F / 190º C for 10 minutes. Place a foil on the baking sheet without touching the top of the batter if possible, during baking.
3. Take crust out and load with chopped kale and then Missir wot lentils and cheese of choice
4. Spray water on the edges and bake for another 8-10 minutes.
5. Take pizza out, top with fresh herbs. Let sit for a minute before slicing.
6. Best served hot.

Chapter Four: Ethiopian Dessert Recipes

Pumpkin Spice Dabo Kolo (Ethiopian Pumpkin Spice Ricotta Donuts)

Serves: 4

Ingredients:

- 2 medium-large eggs
- 1 ½ tablespoons butter (softened)
- ½ cup honey
- ½ tablespoon pumpkin spice
- ½ pound ricotta cheese
- ½ cup unbleached all-purpose flour
- ¼ teaspoon fine sea salt
- vegetable oil (for frying)

Method:

1. In medium sized bowl, whisk ricotta cheese until creamy. Add eggs and whisk well. Whisk in the pumpkin spices, flour, salt and butter.
2. Add oil to a deep-frying pan (or a wok) to about ½ inch up the side of the pan. Heat oil to 350-360 degrees or until a bit of the dough instantly rises to the surface when added.
3. Add dough to pan, 1 tablespoon a time, pushing it off with a spoon or spatula. When it turns golden brown on one side, turn to brown other side, until puffed into small balls.
4. Transfer dough with a slotted spoon to a paper lined baking sheet and allow to cool slightly.

5. To serve, arrange on a platter and drizzle with the honey. Enjoy!

Ethiopian Ras El Hanout Crescent Cookies

Yield: 60 pieces

Ingredients:

- 250 grams pastry flour
- 225 grams cold butter (cubed)
- 150 grams ground almonds
- 125 grams dark chocolate (minimum 60% cocoa)
- 100 grams sugar
- 2 medium egg yolks
- 1 teaspoon *ras el hanout* *
- pastry flour (to work)
- parchment paper (for baking)

Method:

1. First, combine the flour, ground almonds and sugar in a large bowl and make a well in the center. Add the egg yolks and distribute the butter and ras el hanout over the top.
2. Mix everything together using a pastry blender or two forks, then quickly knead with hands to form a smooth dough. Wrap with plastic wrap and refrigerate for 30 minutes.
3. Preheat the oven to 160°C (approximately 325°F). Line a baking sheet with parchment paper.
4. Transfer the dough to a floured surface and divide into 4 equal portions. Shape each portion into a roll about 2-3 cm (approximately ¾-1 inch) in diameter. Cut each roll into 1 cm (approximately 3/8 inch) thick slices and shape into crescents.

5. Place the crescents onto the prepared baking sheet and bake for 10-12 minutes, until lightly golden. Remove from the oven and let cool.
6. Coarsely chop the chocolate and melt in a double boiler or heatproof bowl over a saucepan of simmering water. Transfer the melted chocolate to a freezer bag with the corner tip cut off and drizzle the chocolate over the cooled cookies.

* Ras El Hanout:

Ingredients:

- 1 ½ teaspoons coriander seeds
- 1 ¼ teaspoons ground cinnamon
- 1 teaspoon paprika
- ¾ teaspoon cumin seeds
- ½ teaspoon crushed chili flakes
- ½ teaspoon ground cardamom
- ½ teaspoon ground ginger
- ½ teaspoon ground turmeric

Method:

1. Toast coriander and cumin seeds in a small skillet over medium heat, stirring occasionally, until aromatic and slightly darkened, about 4 minutes.
2. Transfer to a spice mill and let cool.
3. Add crushed red pepper flakes. Process until finely ground. If you don't have a spice mill, use a pestle & mortar. Transfer to a small bowl.
4. Add remaining ingredients and mix.

5. Can be made 1 month ahead. Store airtight at room temperature. Makes approximately 2-3 tablespoons

Ethiopian Destaye Pierogies

Serves: 24 pieces

Ingredients:

Filling:

- 1 ½ ounces (about ¼ cup) raisins—regular, golden, or a mix
- 1 ½ ounces (about ¼ cup) shelled whole pistachios
- 1 ounce (about ½ cup) shredded unsweetened coconut
- 1 pinch kosher salt
- 1 ounce (about 1/3 cup) sliced almonds
- 1 tablespoon unsalted butter
- 1 tablespoon dark brown sugar
- ½ teaspoon ground cardamom

Oat dough:

- 2 medium-large eggs (divided)
- 3 tablespoons (1 ½ ounces; 43 grams) unsalted butter (melted and slightly cooled)
- 1 ¼ cups (4 ¼ ounces; 120 grams) oat flour
- 1 cup (4 ¼ ounces; 120 grams) unbleached all-purpose flour
- 1 tablespoon water
- 1 tablespoon granulated sugar
- ½ cup (4 ounces; 113 grams) sour cream or plain Greek yogurt (any fat percentage)
- ¼ teaspoon kosher salt

Method:

Make the filling:

1. Start by toasting the coconut in a large skillet over low heat, stirring and shaking the pan frequently and watching carefully as the shreds darken from off-white to pale beige. Remove the pan from the heat as soon as you see spots where the coconut is turning mahogany brown. Pour the coconut into the bowl of a mini food processor.
2. Add the pistachios and almonds to the pan and return to low heat. Toast the nuts, again stirring and shaking the pan to get equal heat distribution. As soon as the almonds get a bit of brown on them and you can smell the toastiness in the pan, remove from the heat and add the nuts to the mini food processor.
3. Add the raisins to the food processor. Pulse a few times to coarsely chop the nuts and raisins.
4. Put the skillet back over low heat and melt the butter. Add the brown sugar and cardamom and stir continuously until the sugar dissolves into a granular liquid, about 1 minute. Pour the chopped-up contents of the food processor back into the skillet and stir to coat evenly with the spiced sugar.
5. Remove from the heat one last time, scrape the filling into a bowl and let cool to room temperature.
6. Filling can be made up to 1 week ahead. Store in an airtight container at room temperature.

Make the dough:

1. Whisk 1 large egg, sour cream or yogurt, butter, sugar, and salt in a bowl. Whisk the oat and all-purpose flours together in a large bowl. Gently stir the wet ingredients

into the flour. The dough will initially be very dry and shaggy, seeming as if it will never come together, keep stirring, and it will pull itself into shape.

2. Once the dough starts to come together, press and smash it against the sides of the bowl with your palms, picking up dough bits and essentially kneading it within the bowl until it forms a ball.

3. Tip the dough and any remaining shaggy flakes out onto a clean work surface. Knead until smooth, about 1 minute. Cover the dough with the bowl and let rest 15 minutes.

4. Make an egg wash by whisking the remaining large egg and water in a small bowl.

Assemble the pierogis:

1. Line a rimmed baking sheet with waxed paper or parchment paper.

2. Divide the rested dough into 4 equal pieces with a bench scraper or knife. Set aside 3 dough pieces and cover with the mixing bowl. Roll the remaining dough as thinly as possible into a rough 8- by 12-inch rectangle.

3. Using a 3-inch round cookie cutter, cut out 6 rounds of dough. If the dough isn't quartered evenly, you may get 5 rounds from one piece and 7 from another. Resist the temptation to re-roll dough scraps for additional rounds. It seems wasteful, but the dough won't be as tender the second time around.

4. Place 1 teaspoon filling into the center of each dough round. Using your finger, swipe a very scant amount of egg wash—just a light touch—around the dough edge.

5. Fold into a half-moon shape: Either fold the dough over the filling on the work surface or gently cup the pierogi in your hand in a U shape.

6. Gently but firmly seal the pierogi by pinching and squeezing the edges together with your thumb and pointer finger. Start with one pinch at the top, then move to one "corner" of the pierogi and pinch along the edge back to the top. Repeat on the opposite side to finish sealing the pierogi.

7. Transfer to the baking sheet and repeat with remaining dough rounds and filling.

8. At this point you can freeze the pierogis on the baking sheet until solid, then transfer to a zip-top bag or vacuum-seal for storage up to 3 months. Or you can cover with plastic wrap or a non-terrycloth towel and store at room temperature for 1 hour, or in the refrigerator for up to 3 hours before cooking. Or you can cook them right away.

Cook your pierogis:

To boil fresh or frozen pierogis:

Bring a pot of water to a boil over medium-high heat (fill the pot with approximately 1-quart water for every 6 pierogis). Add pierogis and cook until floating, about 2 to 3 minutes for fresh and 4 to 5 minutes for frozen.

To boil fresh or boiled pierogis:

Heat 1 tablespoon canola or vegetable oil, or melt 1 tablespoon unsalted butter in a skillet over medium heat. Add as many pierogis as will fit in the skillet in a single layer without crowding. Cook until pierogis are brown and crispy, about 2 minutes per side. Repeat with additional oil or butter and pierogis.

To deep-fry fresh or frozen pierogis:

Use an electric deep fryer or a large, high-sided pot filled with at least 2 inches of vegetable or canola oil (fill the pot no more than 1/3 full). Heat oil to 350 degrees. Add pierogis and cook until golden brown, about 3 minutes for fresh and 5 minutes for frozen—frying time may vary based on your equipment.

Line a baking sheet with paper towels. Transfer pierogis to the baking sheet and cool for 1 minute before serving.

Ethiopian Lentil Sambusa

Serves: 25

Ingredients:

Niter kibbeh:

- 250 g of unsalted butter
- 4 black cardamom pods (crushed)
- 2 garlic cloves (sliced)
- 1 shallot (finely diced)
- 1 knob of ginger (sliced)
- 1 cinnamon stick
- 1 teaspoon cumin seeds
- 1 teaspoon fenugreek seeds
- 1 teaspoon coriander seeds
- 1 teaspoon black peppercorns
- 1 bay leaf

Lentil filling:

- 300 ml of vegetable stock
- 150 g of brown lentils
- 2 garlic cloves (minced)
- 1 medium-large onion (finely diced)
- 1 tablespoon of berbere spice
- 1 teaspoon ginger paste
- salt to taste

Dough:

- 250 g of plain flour
- 100 ml of water
- 1 teaspoon salt

To fry the sambusas:

- vegetable oil, for deep fat frying

Method:

1. Start by placing the ingredients for the niter kibbeh in a pan and simmer over a very low heat for 20 minutes. Once the butter solids are starting to caramelize into a beurre noisette, take off the heat and strain through a muslin cloth or coffee filter into a bowl.
2. To make the lentil filling, heat 2 tablespoons of niter kibbeh in a pan and fry the diced onion and berbere on a low heat until soft.
3. Add the ginger and garlic and fry for a further minute.
4. Rinse the lentils until the water runs clear, then add them to the pan and top up with 300ml of stock. Leave to simmer for 50 minutes to 1 hour. Check the seasoning, then transfer the mixture to a tray or plate to cool down quickly.
5. Place all the ingredients for the dough into a bowl, along with 2 tbsp of the niter kibbeh, and mix with a fork until a dough starts to come together.
6. Tip out onto a floured surface and knead for 5 minutes. Place the dough in a lightly oiled bowl and cover with a damp tea towel for half an hour.
7. Divide the pastry into 30g balls and leave them under a cloth as you work to prevent them drying out.
8. Roll a ball into a 2mm thick circle, then cut the circle in half. Add 1 teaspoon of filling to the middle of each semicircle, equidistant between the rounded edge, the cut side and the two corners. Bring the bottom corner up over the filling to cover, then fold the top corner down to create a neat triangle.

9. Pinch the open edges of the dough together, using a little water to help seal the dough if needed. Repeat the process until you have 24–26 sambusas.
10. Preheat a pan of oil or a deep-fryer to 180°C.
11. Fry the sambusas in batches until bubbled up and golden for about 45–60 seconds before draining on kitchen paper.
12. The sambusas can be served hot or at room temperature.

Injera Bread Pudding

Serves: 9

Ingredients:

- ½ loaf sweet egg bread like challah or brioche, cut into 2-inch cubes (about 5 to 6 cups)
- 2 medium-large eggs (beaten)
- 2 cups milk
- 2 tablespoons (1/4 stick) unsalted butter (more for greasing pan)
- 1 teaspoon vanilla extract
- 1/3 cup sugar
- pinch salt (to taste)

Method:

1. Heat your oven to 350 degrees. In a small saucepan over low heat, warm milk, butter, vanilla, sugar and salt. Continue cooking just until butter melts; cool. Meanwhile, butter a 4-to-6-cup baking dish and fill it with cubed bread.
2. Add eggs to cooled milk mixture and whisk; pour mixture over bread. Bake for 30 to 45 minutes, or until custard is set but still a little wobbly and edges of bread have browned.
3. Serve warm or at room temperature. Enjoy!

Ethiopian French Press and Coconut Flour Bundt Cakes - Gluten Free Diary Free

Serves: 24

Ingredients:

For the cake:

- 3 medium-large organic egg whites
- 2 medium-large organic eggs
- 2 teaspoons baking powder
- 1 cup of diary (we used coconut milk- you can use ordinary cow's milk)
- 1 tablespoon french press coffee (this method results in a subtler coffee taste as opposed to an espresso)
- ¾ cups organic coconut flour
- ½ teaspoon bicarbonate of soda
- ½ teaspoon salt
- 1/3 cup *nectacot jam or honey* *

For the glaze:

- 2 teaspoons coffee
- ¾ cup nectacot jam
- ¼ coconut oil

Method:

For the cake:

1. First, preheat your oven to 180 C / 350 F.
2. Mix eggs, egg whites, milk, jam OR honey, 1 tablespoon coffee in a bowl with a hand blender until fluffy.
3. In a separate bowl, mix remaining ingredient.

4. Combine the second bowl's ingredients to the wet mix, should be well combined, but not over mixed.
5. Grease bundt pan well. I used a mini bundt pan making 12 bundt cakes.
6. Spoon mixture in to the bundt baking tray and bake for 40 – 45 mins until golden brown.
7. Allow to fully cool down before removing from the pan.
8. Pour/spoon the nectacot glaze over the bundt cakes before serving.

For the glaze:

1. Combine jam, coffee and coconut oil and whisk lightly. If it is too runny place your sauce in the freezer for a few mins to thicken slightly.

Nectacot Jam:

Ingredients:

- 3 kg nectacot fruit cleaned and halved
- 2 kg sugar
- vanilla pods

Method:

1. Combine the fruit, sugar and vanilla pods into a pot. No water is necessary for this recipe.
2. Boil the mixture and skim the 'scum' off of it whilst it is cooking.
3. Cook the mixture for 45 mins or until it sets on a cool surface.
4. Stir the mixture and allow it to cool.

Ethiopian Griddle Cakes

Serves: 10

Ingredients:

For the griddle cakes:

- 2 teaspoons cumin seeds, toasted and ground
- 1 ½ tablespoons honey
- 1 sweet onion
- 1 teaspoon cinnamon
- 1 cup Greek yogurt (plain, full fat)
- 1 tablespoon brown sugar
- 1 cup red lentils
- ½ cup long grain white rice
- ½ cup walnuts (unsalted)
- ½ to 1 ½ teaspoons cayenne (depending on your heat tolerance)
- ¼ cup black rice
- ¼ teaspoon ground ginger
- 1 medium egg (if needed)
- 1-2 tablespoons flour (if needed)
- niter kibbeh (recipe below)

For the niter kibbeh:

- 1-pound unsalted butter
- 1 small-medium onion (chopped)
- 1/8 teaspoon fresh ground nutmeg
- 4 cloves
- 1 ½ teaspoons fenugreek seeds
- 1 cinnamon stick
- ¾ teaspoon freshly ginger (grated)

- 3 cloves garlic (smashed)
- 4 cardamom pods (smashed)
- ½ teaspoon turmeric

Method:

For the griddle cakes:

1. Put the lentils and both kinds of rice in a pot, cover with water, and bring to a boil over medium-high heat. Reduce heat and cover the pot, simmering for about 25 minutes adding water if necessary. Do not worry if they aren't cooked all the way—you don't want them all the way cooked. And do not worry if the lentils are more done than the rice—the textural variation is lovely and it all gets blitzed in the food processor later. Remove from heat and drain, then return to the warm pot and stir until any remaining water has been evaporated. Set aside.

2. In a food processor, pulse the walnuts until they are a relatively fine ground. Remove to a small bowl and set aside.

3. Add raw onion to food processor (no need to clean it or anything) and run it until you have a thick onion soup-ish texture. Remove the raw onion to the stovetop and sauté it in a small pan over medium heat until most of the water has been evaporated and the onion has lost its "edge," 5 minutes or so.

4. Return rice, lentils, onion, walnuts and remaining spices to the food processor and run until the mixture is relatively even-textured.

5. Heat a generous amount of niter kibbeh in a sauté pan over medium heat. Add a tablespoon of the batter to the pan and fry for about 5 minutes per side, until crispy and brown on both sides. Remove to a paper towel-lined plate

and let cool. Test it out. If it holds together okay, carry on. If not, add an egg or a tablespoon or two of flour and try again.

6. When your batter is the right consistency, shape it into patties (3 to 4 inches in diameter) and fry in the niter kibbeh. Make sure to wipe the sauté pan clean after each batch and add fresh niter kibbeh. Serve with Greek yogurt mixed with honey.

For the niter kibbeh:

1. Melt butter over low heat. When completely melted, add all the remaining ingredients and cook on the lowest temperature possible for about an hour. Feel free to skim any accumulated solids off the top of the pan if you like. Strain through a cloth (I use left-over diaper cloths because I don't have cheese cloth).

Note:

- This makes a lot of niter kibbeh. Alternative uses for the glorious stuff: Add a couple tablespoons to rice or lentils when cooking. Dollop on top of steamed vegetables. Spread it on toast topped with sardines and tomato (okay, that last one may just be me). The possibilities are endless! It is SO easy to make and it smells/tastes so delicious. It can seriously take your cauliflower to places you didn't even know existed.

Ethiopian Truffles

Serves: 20 cookies

Ingredients:

For the pastry:

- 2 cups flour
- 1 cup butter
- ½ teaspoon vanilla extract
- ½ teaspoon vanilla bean powder
- ½ confectioners sugar

For the filling:

- 8 ounces semi-sweet chocolate chips
- 2 medium egg whites
- 1 2/3 cups almonds (blanched)

Method:

For the pastry:

1. In large bowl of a mixer cream the butter with the sugar until smooth. Add the vanillas. On low speed add the flour a ½ cup at a time.
2. Once all flour is in and dough is in a uniform ball shape. Place in a piece of wax paper and flatten into a large disk.
3. Place in the refrigerator to chill and rest.

For the filling:

1. In a bowl of a food processor finely grind the almonds and chocolate. Place into a bowl and mix in the egg whites.

Assembling Truffles:

1. Divide the dough in 20 similar sized balls. Flatten a piece in the palm of your hand that is big enough to a small 2 teaspoon bit of the chocolate filling.
2. Close the dough all around the filling and place on a parchment lined cookie sheet. If the dough sticks, then dust your hands with a bit of confectioners sugar.
3. Place the cookies 1 inch apart on cookie sheet and refrigerate for about 20 minutes. During this time preheat the oven to 375 degrees. Bake the cookies for 15 to 20 minutes or until they are lightly golden.
4. Let cool completely then dust with confectioners sugar.
5. Enjoy. Great with a cup of coffee or tea.

Ethiopian Honey Wine

Serves: 4-6

Ingredients:

- 2 cups water
- 1/3 cup honey
- 1 (750-ml) bottle white wine (Use a light, mildly sweet white wine such as a riesling, soave or pinot grigio).

Method:

1. In a small saucepan, heat the water and honey over low flame, stirring until the honey is completely dissolved. Remove from heat and chill completely.
2. Pour the honey water and wine together into a decorative glass decanter, mix together and serve lightly chilled.

Conclusion

Again, I truly wish to thank you for purchasing this book.

Ethiopian food is without a doubt some of the world's most unique and delicious. In addition to its amazing dishes, incredible stews, and amazing combination of spices, Ethiopian cuisine offers a *cultural experience* that revolves around how food should be served and shared with friends and family.

Eating Ethiopian food is a truly social event – a shared experience that involves everyone around the table eating and smiling.

With all this in mind, it is important to remember that great food starts with great ingredients, and that you should never be afraid to season your dish. So, take your first steps into Ethiopian cooking with open arms and an open mind, and I can promise that you will not leave disappointed.

So, thank you, and enjoy the journey!

Other Books by Grizzly Publishing

"Jamaican Cookbook: Traditional Jamaican Recipes Made Easy"

https://www.amazon.com/dp/B07B68KL8D

"Brazilian Instant Pot Cookbook: Delicious Pressure Cooked Meals Made Fast and Easy"

https://www.amazon.com/dp/B078XBYP89

"Norwegian Cookbook: Traditional Scandinavian Recipes Made Easy"

https://www.amazon.com/dp/B079M2W223

"Casserole Cookbook: Delicious Casserole Recipes From Around The World"

https://www.amazon.com/dp/B07B6GV61Q

Lightning Source UK Ltd.
Milton Keynes UK
UKHW022028210719
346566UK00025B/579/P